NEXTMAPPING™:

Anticipate, Navigate and Create the Future of Work

SECOND EDITION

Cheryl Cran

AUTHORS PLACE
— PRESS —

Published by Authors Place Press
9885 Wyecliff Drive, Suite 200
Highlands Ranch, CO 80126
Authorsplace.com

ISBN: 978-1-62865-713-5

*To my husband, my best friend, and my biggest supporter, Reg.
You are the "wind beneath my wings."*

*And to all of my clients around the world who have read my
books, been in my audiences, and have taken action on the
ideas and solutions that have been ignited in your minds.*

*And to the leaders just like you who are constantly learning, growing,
and sharing your energy and leadership with your teams. YOU
inspire me, and I truly believe that together we can change the world.*

CONTENTS

ABOUT AUTHOR

Cheryl Cran is the founder of NextMapping™/NextMapping.com and the CEO of parent company Synthesis at Work Inc.

Recognized as the #1 Future of Work influencer by Onalytica, and in the top ten of future of work influencers by Catalant.

Cheryl is the author of 7 books, including, "The Art of Change Leadership – Driving Transformation in a Fast-Paced World" (Wiley 2015), "101 Ways to Make Generations X, Y, and Zoomers Happy at Work" (2010), and others, including "Leadership Mastery in the Digital Age" (2013), "The Control Freak Revolution" (2008), "50 Ways to Lead and Love It" (2001), "Say What You Mean – Mean What You Say" (2000).

Cheryl's future of work thought leadership has been featured in publications such as Washington Post, Huff Post, Forbes, IABC Magazine, Law Magazine, Metro New York, Entrepreneur Magazine, Readers Digest, CBS Online, NBC Online, CNBC, Fox Online, and more.

For over two decades, Cheryl has built a reputation for delivering extraordinary value to clients that include AT&T, Bell Mobility, Omnitel, Gartner, British Telecomm, Manulife, as well as mid-sized companies and entrepreneurs in industries that include technology, health, agriculture, finance, insurance, and more.

NextMapping™ was developed as our proprietary business solution brand that encompasses all of Cheryl's work and research on the future of work and the leadership needed to navigate change in the workplace. It's time not only to hear about the future but also to use NextMapping™ to get there!

A people-first focus and culture along with technology in the workplace must be used to prepare for the future with a focus on how technology can enhance outcomes for people.

The common theme of all of Cheryl's life's work is a "people-first" focus and digital second approach to create a more human future, helping companies build the leadership capacity needed to "change the world through business."

PREFACE

THE POWER OF NEXTMAPPING™

We are living in crazy times, everywhere we turn there are new events that cause us to shake our heads and wonder, "What's going on?" It can be difficult to stay inspired or consistently lead others with inspiration toward a positive and optimistic future.

That's why having tools and resources to help anticipate changes and then know what to do about it are crucial to these fast-changing times.

I have always been someone who could "see the future," and I have been intrigued by finding patterns in the past and in human behavior and then seeing potentialities for the future. However, where I struggled in my early career was with the "how to get to the future I wanted to create." I could "see" it, but I didn't necessarily have a plan for how to get to the future I wanted to create. That challenge in my early career created a burning desire in me to create systems for others and myself on how to convert what we "see" into "what we want to create."

Today, many years later, NextMapping™ helps turn future visions into creative solutions and actionable plans for myself and for our clients.

My studies in human behavior, psychology, organizational change, and leadership have directed me toward being deeply interested in helping people create an inspiring and successful future.

After two decades of working with leaders and teams globally, I found that people inherently want to do well at work, want to succeed, and want to create a fulfilling life. When my team and I began to look at rebranding what we do and how we can elevate our services for our clients, we discovered a few things.

Firstly, the branding company we worked with interviewed our clients and found that they saw our consulting firm as being unique in that we don't just see and predict the future; we help organizations and people to create it and get there successfully.

Secondly, the branding company was able to take what we have been doing for clients over the years and succinctly put into one word: NextMapping™.

The power of NextMapping™ is that our proprietary process works in a one-on-one coaching basis, consulting process, or as a keynote or workshop. The NextMapping™ system encompasses the entire spectrum of ideation, creative solutions, and implementation.

Great ideas and staying ahead of the competition requires execution of great ideas. Many leaders and teams cite lack of time for the main reason they ignore the trends or focus on innovation. However, with NextMapping™ you can integrate the ideas and actions into your current strategy, AND you can inspire your teams to make it a cultural imperative.

NEXTMAPPING™ 2020 AND BEYOND

One year ago, we published the original version of this book, and what a difference a year makes! In these fast-changing times, so much changes in one year—for example AI has now infiltrated more of our everyday lives and our work. In the past year, companies like Survey Monkey have added AI in the form of sentiment analysis for its surveys. Sentiment analysis allows for AI to determine the "mood" of respondents to survey questions. This added feature provides additional customer and employee insights and helps to better understand how respondents feel about specific issues, services, or products.

In 2019, Artificial Intelligence has progressed in a number of ways. Natural language processing being used for closed captions on videos and near-real-time transcription of audio and video through companies such as rev.com. Natural language processing through AI also provides foreign subtitles and language translations.

Natural language processing is also being used in customer service to generate reports and market summaries and is offered by companies like Attivio, Automated Insights, Cambridge Semantics, Digital Reasoning, Lucidworks, Narrative Science, and SAS.

In the past year, there has been greater uptake of and improvements in speech recognition. Siri is just one of the systems that can understand you. Every day, more and more systems are created that can transcribe human language, reaching hundreds of thousands through voice-response interactive systems and mobile apps. Companies offering speech recognition services include NICE, Nuance Communications, OpenText, and Verint Systems.

Machine learning is being used to better predict buying and customer behaviors. Companies like Google, SAS, Skytree, and Adext are using real AI and machine learning to find the most profitable audience or demographic for any ad.

In the past year, Delta Air Lines has <u>introduced facial recognition</u> for faster boarding of international travelers at specific airports in the US. Seventy-two percent of customers prefer facial recognition to standard boarding at ATL F, the first curb-to-gate biometric terminal in the US. Biometrics is set to transform many processes in the rest of 2019 and in 2020. This technology can identify, measure, and analyze human behavior and physical aspects of the body's structure and form. It allows for more natural interactions between humans and machines, including interactions related to touch, image, speech, and body language recognition, and is big within the market research field. 3VR, Affectiva, Agnitio, FaceFirst, Sensory, Synqera, and Tahzoo are all biometrics companies transforming machine/human interactions in the next year. Robotic processes automation uses scripts and methods that copy and automate human tasks to support business processes. RPA with AI saves people from devoting hours to mechanical and repetitive tasks. It further frees up people to focus more on the management of work versus the tasks of work. Robotic processes automation is a solution that lets you make the most of your human talent and move employees into more strategic and creative positions so their actions can really make an impact on the company's growth. We will see further technological advances in 2020 and beyond, and the biggest opportunity is for companies to focus on providing the tools and resources for people. NextMapping™ the future of "humans" is the biggest focus for us in 2020 and beyond. Companies that focus on building leadership abilities, upskilling and reskilling workers, and helping people change mindsets and make changes to be able to readily adapt will be key themes 2020 and beyond. This second edition provides updated research and tools to anticipate, navigate, and create the future of work.

PART ONE

ANTICIPATE THE FUTURE OF WORK

CHAPTER ONE

THE FUTURE OF WORK IS NOW- ARE WE READY?

"The future is ours to win but to get there we can't stand still."
Barack Obama

Imagine that in the future, you wake up and look in your mirror that tells you how you slept and what your vitals are, recommends what you should eat that day, advises you on what you should do for exercise, and pep talks you on how wonderful you are. You walk into the kitchen, and your mirror already shared your food recommendations with the autonomous robot chef who 3D prints your breakfast, tells you what happened in world news while you slept, and answers any questions you may have about chores or tasks for the day. Today you choose to go into your shared office space, and you ask your robot to clean the house and prepare dinner for guests you are having over after you return from your workspace.

Your robot ordered your autonomous car that is waiting outside your door—you hop in and tell the car where you are going—the car sets off, and while on your way, you lean back and put on your virtual reality headset to participate in a training on how to better interact with team members.

You arrive at the shared workspace and it's smart enabled, which means you can voice activate any of your requests. Rather than a lobby, there is a vertical garden that supplies fresh organic food to be picked and eaten by anyone, and there is a program to provide food from the vertical garden to underprivileged people.

Everyone in the world has high-speed Internet, and you can connect with remote workers from every country in the world. Drones allow you to share information with other team members in real time, and drones share video and audio records automatically when requested. The entire building is powered by solar and wind and operates at the highest efficiencies. Your mother is in an elderly care community and sends you a holographic message that her elder care robot has been auto upgraded.

At work, you have team meetings with people in real life by hologram, which seems as if they are there in person.

Your coworker robot provides well-being advice by sensing your stress levels and suggests you take a nap or a mindfulness session. You delegate all current problems and creative challenges to be solved to your robot, and while you nap, the robot works away at your problem. You come back refreshed, and you check in on your teammates who are twenty-four hours ahead in time zone—they are sleeping but have left you a holographic message to interact with their coworker robot, and you get the answers you needed. You check on your coworker robot's solutions that you delegated—ask questions and delegate more work to follow through on.

You have been at work for a few hours and now it's time to head home— your coworker robot orders your autonomous car to drive you home. You arrive home and the house is clean, food is prepped and ready, and you are able to sit back and enjoy the drink pre-prepared for you. Your guests arrive, and you suggest playing an interactive game with your robot and holograms of friends from far away. Your friends leave and you wash up for bed—your mirror recaps your health and your choices and tells you how wonderful you are. You climb into your bed and your robot closes the shades, dims the lights, and says goodnight.

Now imagine that while in the workplace you have a team meeting that has been set up and organized using voice technology and automated calendar integrations with either your smart watch or your embedded chip. In preparation for the meeting, AI, natural language processing, and technology integration has brought together every stakeholder's work on specific projects and created a visual. In that integrated visual is the overall project progress shown in percentage images, performance of each stakeholder, and where each is at with commitments and deadlines, and it shows what needs to happen next and who does what. The image of the project's progress is not shown through PowerPoint or Keynote, rather it is projected into any open space and any team member can move the data using swipes and voice commands to help everyone see the data in a variety of forms.

Imagine that AI and sentiment analysis can pick up on the emotions of all members in the meeting and can identify when someone is upset, stressed, or holding back. The meeting lead is a robot that is able to identify when someone needs to express their concerns or thoughts. The robot meeting lead is able to keep the meeting on point, professional, and objective and curtail any personal agendas that may arise. Imagine that decisions are made on "real" data that has been vetted against scientific data and is used for irrefutable information. Imagine that humans cannot manipulate or promote his or her agenda because the data and the robotic oversight ensures objective, truthful, and data-based decisions. Imagine that the humans in the meeting are there to ensure that the focus is on "people first" and that all decisions around changes that are needed are based on "what's best for the client or employee."

Imagine that any task that needs to be delegated from the outcomes of the meeting are delegated to a robot or a system and that the humans in the meeting are the overseers of the delegated tasks. Imagine that the speed of action is increased due to data being able to propose scenarios and that all team members can view those scenarios by donning augmented and virtual reality headsets that show the effect of potential decisions.

Imagine that the workplace has a vibe of more of a social club than a typical workplace. The workplace is built around "work," not jobs, and the work is allocated to the best solution for its completion. Therefore, more work is around specific projects, and people are required to learn how to adapt to ever-changing project teams. Imagine that the skills needed to navigate this new workplace include the ability to interact with both people and machines seamlessly and to leverage the integration of skills between people and robots to greater innovation and collaboration.

Imagine that many of the current world problems are solved such as famine, disease, poverty, and discrimination. Imagine that technology helps to solve some of the human, biased decisions for business and growth and focuses purely on data that supports what's best for humans overall, globally.

The imagined personal future may seem fantastical, however in reality, it is not so far away. The imagined team future is very near, and with innovations in technology such as AI, automation, robotics, and more, we are going to see this new world of work within the next few years. The key to the future is to remove the "negative" aspects of humans at work, such as forcing personal agendas, political power moves, and overinflated egos. In the future, I believe technology integration is going to get us/we ready for the future.

If we were to take the imagined futures shared above and look to anticipate the future, we would see the increasing convergence of technology and human behavior. This chapter aims to provide you with insights on the shifts in AI, automation, robotics, people preferences, behaviors, and choices and how they can help you anticipate the future.

In business, competitive advantage is no longer being able to be one step ahead of your competition. Today if you are not anticipating the impact of breakthroughs in multiple industries, products, and services, you are at risk of becoming irrelevant.

Blockbuster ignored the trend toward streaming video and viewed it as a crazy idea and, in fact, exclaimed, "No one will ever stop wanting to buy DVDs." They were wrong.

Kodak ignored digital photos as a trend, and even though Kodak had the inside ability to be Instagram, they soon were impacted by the photo-sharing app swooping in out of the blue to change how photos, and more importantly experiences, are shared.

Taxi services in many cities had enjoyed the monopoly of ride services until a technology company—you might have heard of them—Uber launched a ride-sharing app. Even in cities that have been resisting the Uberization or Lyft impact, they are seeing that client desire is overriding the agenda of keeping the taxi system as is.

Hotel leaders underestimated the desire for people (led by millennials and Gen X) wanting to have authentic travel experiences, which led to the major disruptor Airbnb.

Traditional office spaces and commercial leasing have expected that people will always want to work in square offices in isolation—until WeWork came along and reimagined the workspace of the future, the collaboration and the changing nature of how people want to work.

Restaurants are struggling with attracting people to work for minimum wage, and companies like Uber Eats, DoorDash, and Skip the Dishes are creating a demand for take-out only restaurants as a result. Restaurants in China have automated "robot servers" that take orders, send orders to the kitchen, and bring food to the table.

What do companies like Uber, Airbnb, Instagram, WeWork, and DoorDash have in common?

The leaders of each of these companies had leaders who saw a different future, anticipated new trends, sensed an opening in the cultural mindset, and saw an opportunity to capitalize on the quickly shifting changes of human behavior.

WHY ANTICIPATE?

There is a major difference between a company culture, where the status quo is the norm, and a company that is focused on running the business right in front of them, while also keeping a very open eye to the future, the trends, and the potential disruptions.

A company culture where leaders are simply focused on the business as it is and have become complacent around continuous improvement is very much at risk.

40% of Fortune 500 companies will not exist in the next ten years.

It is predicted that there will be new Fortune 500s to take the place of those that disappear, and at this time, we don't even know what those companies will provide as far as products and services.

Right now, leaders and teams all need to be futurists anticipating and staying focused on the shifts in human behavior, emerging technologies, as well as the trends shaping rapid upcoming change.

When we look at anticipating the future, there are two areas to focus on:

1. The impact of robots, automation, and AI on life and work.
2. Trends on people preferences, human behaviors, lifestyle choices, and work choices.

Right now, if your business or role involves repetitive tasks, it is likely you have already or will be impacted by robotics and automation. It is irrefutable that we need to expand our perspective to seeing that robots, AI, and automation are infiltrating all industries and everyday life.

Before we look at robotics/automation/Artificial Intelligence (AI) / Augmented Reality (AR)/Virtual Reality (VR), let's explore what each of these technologies does.

Robotics is where a task or command is assigned or delegated to a robot to carry out the task—a simple example would be a Roomba, a self-driving vacuum cleaner. Automation is any task that can be automated through programming, such as drip campaigns through email or automatic upgrades of an operating system or a manufacturing process of filling containers.

Augmented Reality, abbreviated as AR, is a technology that superimposes virtual elements onto the physical environment. As the name suggests, it actually augments artificially generated components, which enhances the user experience. Remember Snapchat filters? On the other hand, Virtual Reality, abbreviated as VR, is a technology that blocks users off the physical world and immerses them in a different, virtual surrounding altogether. In other words, it tricks and manipulates the user's mind to believe a 3D computer-generated environment as real. Both AR and VR hold immense promise and potential in 2020 and beyond.

Let's now take a look at how some of these technological innovations are impacting various industries:

Healthcare – Robots in Japan have been created that are called "carebots." These robots are able to lift and move patients and are poised to become the norm in hospitals globally. One of the biggest challenges for nurses and healthcare professionals is lifting patients—it's a major cause of injury on the job. If we look at how carebots can literally do the heavy lifting, then it means that healthcare professionals can focus on what they do best—providing superior human-based health care to patients.

Automation is also happening at the administrative level in healthcare. According to the statistics available in McKinsey Quarterly, 36% of the healthcare tasks—mostly managerial and back-office—are amenable to automation. The benefits of robotic process automation in healthcare include increased operational efficiency, productivity, and cost-savviness. In 2020 and beyond, we are going to see an increase in virtual health care—companies such as <u>Copeman</u> in Canada provide virtual doctor appointments for patients anywhere and virtually at any time. In the past year, AI was better at <u>diagnosing illness than a doctor</u>, and AI is quickly improving <u>biomedical imaging</u> for faster illness diagnosis.

Meanwhile, <u>AR is being used to help doctors</u>, surgeons, and patients facing medical professionals to better empathize when communicating with a patient.

Manufacturing – Robots in manufacturing have been in place perhaps the longest. Car manufacturers have been using robots on the assembly line for over a decade. Robots in manufacturing have expanded to robots like OTTO that are self-driving couriers. OTTO can deliver parts; where a person would have spent time moving materials around the factory floor or getting a restful night's sleep, the robots are on 24/7 and act as couriers, saving time for people to spend on more productive tasks.

The cost of the technology is cost-effective, and OTTO Motors plans to put robots into the world's dullest, deadliest, and dirtiest jobs. This is where the company sees them having the most profound and positive effects on our lives.

Exoskeleton technology is transforming the safety of warehouse workers as well as any profession where there is lifting or risk for lower body injury. Companies such as <u>Lockheed Martin</u> have created a defense exoskeleton, and companies such as Walmart, Home Depot, and Amazon have been using the <u>exoskeleton for their warehouse workers</u> for the past year or so. AR in a warehouse is quite promising for item picking. By guiding warehouse employees through order-picking operations, handheld mobile devices and smart glasses with augmented reality software reduce time expenditures and the error rate. What's more, such guidance can noticeably shorten training for new employees and let them work efficiently from the very start.

Finance – Most of the robotics and automation in finance are <u>chatbots or digital assistants</u> and are either cloud-based or in the shape of robots and humanoids. Additional automation breakthroughs in finance are related to back-end operations or fraud prevention.

The Royal Bank of Scotland introduced Luvo, an advanced AI bot to assist customers. Bank of America introduced Erica, a text and voice chatbot to help clients with routine operations and mobile banking. Bank of Tokyo has Nao, a multilingual assistant with access to nineteen languages and also has camera and microphone capabilities to interact with clients. CoiN, or contract intelligence, is being used by JPMorgan Chase as an analyzer of documents with the ability to extract relevant clauses. ICICI bank, one of India's major private lenders, became the first in the country to adopt software robotics, also known as robotic process automation (RPA), on a large scale. The operations department deployed around 200 robotics software programs, which helped in processing close to one million transactions daily. AI grows more sophisticated and ubiquitous each day. <u>Artificial intelligence</u> is already automating financial services that used to be performed by humans, and that trend shows no sign of slowing. AI is being used in risk assessment, fraud detection and protection, trading, and even financial advice. The future belongs to financial enterprises that embrace and leverage AI to make maximum use of its potential. Banking has undergone rapid change in the last decade, especially in the area of mobile banking. In 2019, most people banked through their smartphones instead of going to a bank branch. By 2023, it's estimated that dedicated AI chips will become standard in most smartphones. Mobile technology will play an even bigger role in the future of banking. Collections are changing too with AI helping increase successful collections through companies such as <u>Katabat</u>.

Insurance – Chatbots and AI to help in claims risk and real-time underwriting are just a few of the innovations affecting insurance. Companies such as Lemonade are completely transforming the insurance industry. The entire Lemonade customer experience is app-based, although buyers can also start the process through a web-based wizard that is driven by wizard-like interactions with a chatbot named Maya. Maya asks buyers questions about their insurance needs and based on the responses creates a policy tailored to their needs. Once a customer's policy is in effect, the Lemonade app is used to manage the policy and file claims. Changes to the policy, such as increases or decreases to coverage limits, can be made with a few taps, and documentation for claims, such as photographs, can be submitted without offline human interaction. Lemonade uses AI to evaluate claims and boasts that it set the world record for settling a claim from approval to payout—three seconds. Insurance companies are quickly adapting to the rise of workers wanting to work remotely. Technology platforms are being innovated to integrative solutions across the entire range of insurance processes such as claims, underwriting, and risk assessment.

Retail – Lowe's introduced LoweBot, a NAVii™ autonomous retail service robot by Fellow Robots, in eleven Lowe's stores throughout the San Francisco Bay area. LoweBot was rolled out over a seven-month period in San Jose, California, and will continue to explore how robots can meet the needs of both customers and employees. Sephora uses AI to engage customers through the online store and advises customers when it is time to buy new items by tracking customer spending history. Sephora also pioneered the Virtual Artist, which allows customers to "try on" makeup using virtual technology.

Many of us have used the automated self-serve checkouts at Target, Home Depot, and other retailers. Of course, a major technological innovation with all retail is Apple Pay, tap to pay, and, coming soon, paying with Bitcoin. (Bitcoin is currently available at retailers such as Overstock.com, Expedia, and Shopify.)

Drones are essentially flying robots and are in the beginning stages of completely transforming services in businesses as well as human quality of life. Recently, I worked with a client in Florida, where I facilitated a one-and-a-half day event for an award-winning city outside of Miami. This city has been nominated for the <u>Mayors Challenge</u> awarded by Bloomberg due to their innovation track record toward being a smart city of the future. I have worked with the city for two years in a row as the facilitator of their Innovation-focused event where there are guest speakers that include the chief technology dean from University of Miami, consultants on human behavior, and leadership experts.

As part of the facilitation, I polled and included the audience in the presentations throughout the event and had them work in groups on innovation. One of the exercises I gave them was to come up with ten ways a drone could improve services for citizens in their city while also improving their jobs. Some of the ideas they came up with included:

» Drones for surveillance and safety that could be used by police and community police to improve on lowering crime.

» Drones as office couriers moving items between offices and city worker buildings.

» Drones for search and rescue of missing persons.

» Drones to pick up and discard dog waste from neglectful dog owners.

» Drones to provide information to tourists through voice activation.

These are just some of the ideas that the group came up with, and all of them have merit. I predict that many of these ideas will be implemented shortly by this highly innovative group of talented people in the city. Of course, you might be thinking, wait a second, what about the regulations around drones? <u>In 2019 the FAA updated</u> its drone guidelines and security requirements to meet the fast pace of companies and individuals using drones.

What are some ways your company is currently using drones?

What are some ways you could see drones affecting your business?

What are some ways you could see drones impacting your personal life?

Focus on the positive and also the risks and how those risks could be mitigated.

Next, think about what you and your business is doing or could be doing around anticipating the impact of digital transformation overall, including automation, AI, and robots, and ask yourself, What could we do to innovate further with the increasing speed of integration of these technologies?

IF YOU ARE A LEADER WITHIN A COMPANY, ASK YOURSELF:

In what ways could we as a company improve our current use of automation, AI, and robots?

Where are we on the path of digital transformation that includes automation, AI, and robots, and what's our plan to further integrate it into the business?

Are we at risk of losing competitive advantage due to not anticipating the rapid impact that AI, automation, and robots are having on our industry?

How can we as a company leverage AR to help with training or situational awareness around our products or services?

How can we as a company leverage VR to help our workers empathize with our clients or to help provide real-time understanding of client problems?

These questions can help you anticipate the future impact of rapid innovations and speed up your approach to ensuring you are not ignoring the signs of potential opportunity for the future of the business.

IF YOU ARE A TEAM MEMBER WITHIN A COMPANY, ASK YOURSELF:

Am I, as a team member, thinking about the impact of automation, AI, and robots on my job, on my team, and on the company overall?

Do I, as a team member, spend time learning about, investigating, and looking outside my team for clues and insights into how we can innovate further?

Where are we as a team doing really well in regard to adapting to new technologies, and where could we do better?

Can we use AR to help our teams do a better job—such as finding data, picking items in the warehouse, etc.?

Can we use VR to provide simulated scenarios for our teams to learn how to better communicate as a team or how to better serve our clients?

IF YOU ARE AN ENTREPRENEUR OR A FREELANCER, ASK YOURSELF:

Am I so busy, focusing on keeping the lights on and current business, that I am ignoring or not paying attention to potential disruptions in my industry?

Do we have the right people with the right skills or the right partners to help us integrate AI, automation, and robots into our business?

What are the tasks I do on a daily basis that could be automated, improved through AI, or be done by a robot?

How could we add AR features to our offerings to our clients?

How could we use VR to help our clients immerse themselves in the full potential of what our services or products can do for them?

TRENDS ON PEOPLE PREFERENCES, HUMAN BEHAVIORS, LIFESTYLE CHOICES, AND WORK CHOICES.

Now, let's take a look at the second way to anticipate the future, and that is through people and human behavior.

With the increasing impact of digitization on all of our lives, there are patterns emerging that are pointing to a future where now, more than ever before, people are seeking to simplify, increase personal time, and increase meaningful connections with others.

People preferences have dramatically shifted over the past few decades, and generational attitudes of Gen X, millennials and now Gen Z have been moving toward a more human future of more time with family, more flexibility with work, and more meaningful experiences both at work and in daily life. In short, in the fast-paced, digitized reality, more people are seeking ways to be "more human" in their lives and in their work. There is a big focus on "searching for meaning" as technology increases its impact on our lives.

Preferences are shaped by values, and the shifting global values are rapidly impacting people's world views. Take a look at this list on then, now, and the future as it relates to shifting people values:

Then	Now	Future
Stability	Flexibility	Malleability
Loyalty	Commitment	Choice
One job	Multiple jobs	Unlimited jobs
Work	Life then work	Life before work
Individualistic	Teams	Community
Obligated	Options	Abundance
Autocratic	Teams	Interconnected hubs
In office	At a desk	Remote
Work alone	Work in teams	Rotating team projects
One career	Multiple employers	Endless contracts/projects

With the people's shifting values, we can look to predict or anticipate what will be needed in the future as far as services, products, and resources.

For example, if right now your business has a high number of people with "then" values, the approach to innovation may be conservative and focused on protecting the past.

Values are very personal and are shaped by upbringing, culture, and exposure to different worldviews. As each generation learns and grows, values evolve and shape the future.

It's extremely important to be aware of your personal values while also being open and amenable to evolving values taking us into the future. Why? Because if you are rigidly fixed to your values, you will resist change and progress and will subconsciously sabotage efforts to successfully create the future for yourself and others.

Knowing that values shape preferences is highly valuable, as it helps to observe patterns in human behaviors. When anticipating the future of work, knowing human behaviors of people increases the ability to both attract and engage people to work with you.

Having keen insight into people and human behavior allows you to have the advantage of anticipating trends and people's future needs. This in turn helps you to be a better leader, team member, or entrepreneur.

As digitization and technology ramp up, we need to increase our understanding of people and our ability to connect human to human.

Human behavior changes follow shifts in values, so let's take a look at some people's behavior changes over the last decade in both life and work:

Life	Work
Spending more time with family	Working for flexible leaders
Valuing self-care	Choosing companies that care
Having fun experiences	Looking for fun at work
Celebrating life	Value being celebrated at work
Experiencing diversity of cultures	Expecting diversity at work
Binge watching meaningful content	Needing stimulating learning
Connecting with personal community	Creating community at work
Life first before work	Meaningful work is expected
Highly valuing personal growth	Wanting to grow, learn and evolve

All of the above human behaviors point to living and working with more intention, meaning, and purpose. In my book, *101 Ways to Make Generations X, Y, and Zoomers Happy at Work,* published in 2010, I had conducted research on the differing values among the generations. In that book, I predicted a rise in more workers wanting to work remotely, wanting to work on a project basis, and wanting to choose their hours of when to work. This has proven to be the case based on shifting values and human behaviors of Gen X, millennials, and now Gen Z.

Take a look again at the human behavior chart and take a few moments to check off the behaviors that you exhibit. Take the exercise one step further and make a list of your team members or colleagues—which of the life and work behaviors do they exhibit?

Next, ask yourself if your company has adapted to this shift in human behaviors or if you need to think more deeply about these shifts of behavior as you look to create the future of work.

In the well-known Maslow's hierarchy, it was established that there is an ascending order of human needs that guides people to evolutionary growth. To review Maslow's model, it includes:

» Physiological needs, which include food, water, warmth, and rest.

» Safety needs, which include security and safety.

» Belongingness, which includes intimate relationships and friends.

» Esteem needs, which includes prestige and feeling of accomplishment.

» Self-actualization, which includes achieving one's full potential & creativity needs.

If we look at the evolution of human behavior over the decades, we could equate the needs of Maslow's hierarchy to the shifts in behavior.

The generations associated with the last World War and post war are known as the "traditionalists" (born prior to 1946). Their reality was one of rations and lack of jobs, and their main focus was on survival or, on Maslow's' hierarchy, "physiological needs."

Post war would increase human need for survival, protect against potential future war, and focus on safety and security. The generation equated with this timeline is the Baby Boomers or today referred to as Zoomers (more on this later), those born between 1946 and 1964.

The children of the Baby Boomers are Gen X, born between 1965 and 1980, and millennials were born after 1980. Both of these generations' timelines focused on belongingness and esteem on Maslow's hierarchy. Why? Because these generations did not have personal experience of war, and all of their security and safety needs were met by their hard-working Baby Boomer parents. Therefore, the Gen X and millennials evolved to focus on belonging and accomplishments.

Now, as we look to the future, the generations' values are merging—it's not so much about age on the timeline as it is about merging demographic values as technology infiltrated society in the eighties.

We also have the Gen Zs, those born 1990 to date, and their influence is already being felt. The timeline for Gen Zs on the Maslow's hierarchy is a dominant quest for self-actualization.

Each generation evolves and grows beyond the previous generation and impacts cultural values and human behaviors to create a new way of thinking, being, and doing for the future. This means that as an entire population, we are moving up the evolutionary scale toward actualization, community, and a greater chance at better life for all of humanity.

Picture a future where the majority of the seven billion people on the planet are focused on self-actualization and achieving it—this would mean we would be living in a very different reality than we are today. We would have the majority of the population at their full potential and creatively solving the world's problems as a collective.

I have provided a simple view of the impact on evolving human needs and where it is taking us in the future. Here are a few questions to ponder:

Right now, where are you on Maslow's hierarchy?

Do you live a relatively safe and secure life with little disruption and spontaneity?

Do you have meaningful relationships with family and friends?

Do you feel on a daily basis that you are accomplishing something?

Does your life have meaning and a sense of purpose?

Do you feel you have reached and are continually seeking to reach your full potential?

Given the shifts in human values and behaviors, can you see how the changing values will impact your business?

How could you adapt your products and services to be ahead of the curve as it relates to what people are seeking?

Lastly, in this chapter, as we look at anticipating the future based on trends and shifts in people preferences, values, and behaviors, let's take a peek at the lifestyle and work choices that people are making today and what will impact the future.

Lifestyle Choices	**Work Choices**
Life and work intersect	Work anywhere at anytime
Technology integrated into all aspects of life	Leverage tech to work anytime
Live anywhere in the world	Work anywhere in the world
Take a sabbatical to live life at fullest	Work projects rather than hours
Mobile entertainment	Work that entertains
Increase quality of experiences	Work for experiential companies
Live in a walkable city	Conveniences at work
Live in a small town	Use technology to report to work
Share homes, cars and other items	Share offices and work space
Share experiences via social media	Share knowledge via virtual reality
Spend money on experiences	Make money to fund life
Make a contribution to the world	Work for a world changing company
Be a freelancer	Work for multiple companies
Share wealth with family	Choose company that values family

With the current lifestyle and work choices people are making today, we can further look at the impact these lifestyle and work choice "trends" have in anticipating the future of work.

With all of the information provided in this chapter, we could predict that workplaces will need to be more open, flexible, and technology based in order to match up with the values, preferences, and choices that people are making.

We could also predict that workers will choose project work, will choose to work in temporary work spaces as needed, and will choose to work with people of similar values and desires to create a better future for the world.

Below, you will find an infographic overview of this chapter that provides you with an at-a-glance resource of anticipating the future of work by knowing more about the impact of AI, automation, and robotics along with the people preferences, behaviors, and choices and how we can use this information as a predictive tool.

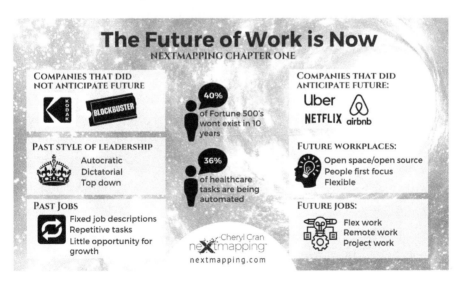

https://nextmapping.com/nextmapping-infographics-download/

CHAPTER TWO

PREDICTING THE FUTURE (A MOVING TARGET)

"You can trust a crystal ball about as far as you can throw it."
Faith Popcorn

If you could predict your personal future, what would you imagine it to be?

Based on where are you are today and looking at your current decisions, are you able to identify your likely future?

Now, add in the uncertainty of current reality—with technology breakthroughs and human behavior shifts, what potential disruptions could you see happening for you?

The reality is that no one can predict the future, although improvements in AI and predictive technology can provide pretty accurate probabilities.

Predictive technology is a body of tools capable of discovering and analyzing patterns in data so that past behavior can be used to forecast likely future behavior. Predictive technologies, which include data mining, neural networks, system modeling, and simulation, have been applied to the study of weather systems, traffic patterns, stock markets, epidemiology, consumer behavior, terrorist activity, and many other areas of study where there can be a significant number of variables.

Predictive technology is increasingly being used for marketing purposes. Many retailers, for example, collect barcode data at their point-of-sale terminals. The raw data can be processed to get predictions about consumer behavior for future campaigns. Amazon.com was one of the earliest online retailers to use predictive technology. The Amazon website compiles lists of merchandise that visitors look at and displays lists of items that customers with similar interests have bought.

Another example of predictive technology is DARPA's proposed Total Information Awareness (TIA) system. The TIA project's ultimate goal is to amass enormous volumes of information about individuals (this collection of data is sometimes called an individual's information signature) from all available sources, to process that data and use predictive technology to identify and avert potential terrorist activity.

In healthcare, a deep learning approach incorporates big data from electronic health records (EHRs) and is able to predict patient outcomes, including possible readmissions, length of stay and, even mortality.

The deep learning predictive tool can analyze more than forty-six billion data points from the EHRs of over 216,000 patients. The predictive analytics of EHRs will revolutionize patient care in the near future.

Technology will continue to enhance our ability to predict the future based on data analytics. For example, I was recently looking at a pair of shoes on my favorite online retail store—I looked at the shoes for about four minutes but decided to think about it before ordering. Later, when I visited my Facebook page, lo and behold, there were the shoes!

Later, I went to Google something and there were the shoes again, and when I went on a completely non-related site for work the shoes were there once again. By tracking my online activities and showing the shoes multiple times, it is quite easily predicted that I will buy those shoes.

Predictive technology is also being used for data security and online protection, and since the Facebook data breach and other breaches, data security will be at the forefront of focus for technology firms now and in the future.

In 2020 and beyond, <u>predictive technology</u> will infiltrate most industries and will be used to help with discerning data points relevant to improving products and services. For example, a company called Clari uses predictive technology to help with sales forecasting and team efficiency. Other companies such as Angoss and Alteryx use predictive technology to help with workflow patterns and improving productivity.

Now to the question: What can we do with current technology and human behavior to predict not only our personal futures but also our company futures?

Although we can't actually predict and "crystal ball" the future, we can leverage insights from the past and change course with present strategies to help steer us to "create the future."

At NextMapping™ we have created the **PREDICT** acronym as a predictive tool that can be used to help us anticipate the future and therefore prepare for the future.

In the companion workbook to this second edition of "NextMapping™ – Anticipate, Navigate, and Create the Future of Work," we provide a full working template to help you leverage the PREDICT model.

Patterns

Recognition

Elevate

Direct

Investigate

Change

Transform

P in the PREDICT acronym is for Pattern, which means in order to predict or anticipate the future we need to look at patterns with a multiple perspectives lens. Patterns in past behavior, patterns in current behavior, and patterns in choices.

As human beings, we are subconsciously repeating patterns over and over again—some patterns serve us, such as patterns of sleeping and eating. Other patterns can harm us, such as smoking and excessive eating.

Patterns in and of themselves cannot help us predict the future, however patterns provide insight into how we can shift personal behaviors, strategies and recognize how those patterns are impacting our choices.

If we refer back to Maslow's hierarchy, we can see that patterns emerge to serve needs. If your need for food is not met, then you may have a pattern of stealing food.

As your needs are met, you elevate to new needs—for example, you could have a need to own a house and once that need is met you now want to own a boat.

Every time we meet a need, it is human nature to seek to evolve to a new desire or a new goal. Eventually as each of us meets all of our material needs and achieves financial security or wealth, we seek to achieve the self-actualization level on Maslow's hierarchy.

For example, you could have a need to pursue success and wealth, and once you have attained that, you have an evolved need to give back or to better contribute your gifts to the world.

Patterns emerge from the past and from memories and can be so ingrained that they reveal themselves in the present when we get triggered. For example, you might have a subconscious memory of being embarrassed whenever you spoke up and now as an adult you hold back in voicing your opinion.

Behavior patterns can either be positive (pattern of sharing with others) or negative (you hold back on sharing), and when predicting the future, we want to be able to identify the positive and negative patterns.

Once we identify all patterns, we can focus on repeating the positive ones and identifying the negative ones.

Personally, one of my patterns is of being recognition driven. When I was a child my father parented with "carrots"—he would provide incentives and rewards for achievements. So, if I got straight A's on my report card, I would get money. When I was thirteen, my Dad told me that if I passed grade eight with A's and B's I could get the dirt bike I had been asking for. Sure enough, I ran home with my report card and proudly showed my Dad, and true to his word, there was my dirt bike waiting with a bow on it. (He anticipated I would get the straight A's and B's and had the bike ready).

You likely have already psychologically analyzed me to know that my pattern of receiving positive recognition has driven me to seek that in my life. Throughout all of my jobs, I strove to go above and beyond, and in my life, I sought recognition for the things I did. The positive of that pattern is that it made me hungry and gave me a strong desire to achieve success, and the negative of that same pattern is that I did not take failure very well.

When I identified that I have a pattern of being recognition driven, I could predict that most endeavors I would undertake will be successful. I can also recognize in advance my pattern of "checking out" in that if I think I am failing and prevent myself from self-sabotaging.

When looking at business patterns, we want to mine the data available to help us identify our ideal clients, our increase in site visits, our increase in purchase periods, the top services that appeal to clients. We also want to look for shifting client behaviors that point to a new pattern of how clients want to engage with our products or services.

Personally, what are some of your patterns of success?

What are some of your patterns of failure?

What are things that "trigger" you (words, actions)?

In order to identify patterns of behavior in your team members, make a list of each of your team members and answer the following questions:

What are his or her patterns of success? (For example, always meets deadlines)

What are his or her patterns of failure or when they do not succeed?

What you have noticed are his or her "triggers" (when they get upset or ineffective).

Pattern identification is highly valuable for strategic planning—by looking at a pattern of customer buying habits, you can identify future product or service opportunities. Or you could identify a pattern of what keeps employees engaged to help determine future employee engagement strategies.

Identifying patterns is an integral exercise in predicting the future for self, in others, and in business.

Some places to look to identify patterns include looking at social media data through hashtags, comments, and engagement. Look for patterns in customer surveys, employee surveys, anecdotal feedback, 360-degree reviews, Google reviews, and Glassdoor reviews.

The power of seeking patterns is found when we program our mindsets and the mindsets of the entire work culture to actively RECOGNIZE patterns in all things on a daily basis.

R in the PREDICT acronym is for Recognize—the more adept you can be at immediate pattern recognition, the quicker you can make a new choice or leverage creative ideas.

Until a pattern is recognized, it is simply background noise buried in the subconscious, and as the pattern is ignored it eventually becomes an obvious sign for change. For example, a leader could have a habit of interrupting his or her team members every time someone speaks. The pattern of interrupting would create tension and cause team members to "shut down" rather than speak. Once the leader sees the pattern either on his or her own or with the help of a coach, they can shift the behavior. However, if the leader never makes the connection between his or her interrupting behavior pattern and the resulting employee disengagement, the leader will continue to struggle with employee engagement.

A leader or team member who has leveraged the ability to "see" patterns in multiple scenarios has the future of work in his or her hands.

When you recognize a pattern, it can literally change your life and can make you smarter. The ability to see patterns is linked with "multiple perspectives intelligence," which I will address later in the book.

Recognizing a pattern is like taking off blinders that you didn't know you were wearing. Your ability to be future ready will be elevated with an increased ability to recognize patterns.

We can recognize patterns in events that regularly repeat themselves—relationship dynamics, trends over time, leadership approaches, and more. Pattern recognition can lead to new discoveries, innovative ideas, and breakthrough concepts.

The evolution of pattern recognition has gone from being able to identify threats to survival for our ancestors to being able to successfully predict the outcomes of investments or health protocols.

The ability to spot existing or emerging patterns is one of the highest intelligence abilities and a critical skill in decision-making. The brain is wired to recognize patterns, but everyone has different ways of seeing patterns.

If you have done personality assessments such as Myers Briggs, DISC, or others, you will know your personality type. The strengths of your personality type would influence how you see patterns.

For example, if you are an analytical personality, you likely have great ability to be "number smart" and see patterns in numbers. If you are a people person, you likely have the ability to be "word smart" and relate through pattern recognition of speech and body language. If you are a driver personality, you likely have risk-taking smarts, which means you can analyze potential risks quickly to make a calculated decision. If you are able to come up with jokes and make people laugh, you are likely humor smart and are able to see patterns in things that are humorous.

People who excel at deciphering human behavior patterns are "people smart," and this skill is *required* to anticipate and navigate the future of work.

If you struggled with answering the above questions I asked about—your patterns of success, your patterns of failure, and what your triggers are —then you may need to spend time elevating your ability to "see" or recognize patterns as a skill.

A great story I like to share on pattern recognition is the proverb from the Tibetan Book of Living and Dying that goes like this:

Chapter One I walk down the street there is a hole in the sidewalk I fall in.

Chapter Two I walk down the street there is a hole in the sidewalk I fall in.

Chapter Three I walk down the street there is a hole in the sidewalk I see it, I fall in.

Chapter Four I walk down the street there is a hole in the sidewalk I see it, I walk around it.

Chapter Five I take another street.

That story is a great allegory on how we can say and do the same things over and over again (definition of insanity) OR we can recognize the pattern, predict several outcomes, and literally take another street.

Just a few days ago I was talking with a client named Christina who is an IT professional for a municipality—we were talking about how in theory, it is easy to implement new technology; what's not easy is getting people to buy in and adopt the new technology.

She shared a personal story of pattern recognition in that many IT folks see technology innovation as positive and necessary. Because of this mindset, the pattern of behavior is to push the technology onto the company with less attention on the users of the technology. Every time IT implements a new technology in a company without involving the stakeholders, I can predict as a consultant that you will have team pushback, slow adoption rate, and low morale.

Christina went on to tell me that she was exactly that IT person who thought her way of implementing IT was the "right" way, and she had an epic fail with a project. What she learned from that fail was leadership gold in that she realized her "pattern" of pushing something through without involving others was going to cause her more work in the end and create animosity with other departments. By recognizing that pattern of behavior, she was able to "take another street." Today, she is a highly respected and successful IT leader who enjoys her work. She is a "change leader" with multiple perspectives and the ability to see patterns and act on those patterns in a way that positively impacts people and the future.

It's important to note that in psychology there is an adage that says, "The way that people do one thing is the way that they do everything."

To leverage pattern recognition to predict the future, here are some questions to consider:

What are the repeatable patterns you recognize in your leaders' leadership approach?

What are the positive patterns you see within your company culture?

What are the customer behavior patterns you see with your clients?

What are the process and service patterns that we have as a company, and are they creating the positive client outcomes we want to achieve?

What are our competitor's patterns when it comes to innovation?

What resources and coaching to our teams on becoming more adept at pattern recognition?

Once we have built the ability to increase our pattern recognition, we have the E in the PREDICT acronym, which stands for Elevates.

Pattern recognition elevates our ability to better predict the future.

Statistics can help us see patterns and help us make informed decisions for the future.

Did you know?

The speed of change is ten times faster than it was a decade ago.

The human brain takes in about thirty-four gigabytes of information daily, enough to overload a laptop in one week.

More than 50% of the global population is under the age of thirty.

By 2020, 46% of the workforce will be millennials.

Video makes up 67% of mobile usage.

By 2025, the workforce will consist mostly of contracted and entrepreneurial workers.

By 2025, 50% of workers will work virtually.

Considering these statistics as patterns, we can use them to elevate our prediction ability.

Let's look at the first statistic that the speed of change is ten times faster than it was a decade ago.

Think back to ten years ago—what were the patterns of life and business at that time?

Some that come to mind include manual calculations, manual labor, strict nine-to-five hours, highly structured job descriptions, male-dominated leadership, traditional values on marriage, traditional views on gender, people stayed in their jobs for many years, the perception that the longer the hours you put in the harder you were perceived to work, clients were loyal to one brand . . . What else?

The patterns of ten years ago were structured, hierarchical, rules based, inflexible, etc.

Today we can see that the changes in the past decade include:

Technological innovation means more jobs requiring technical skills.

Work is becoming more flexible with flextime, freelance, and contract work.

Diversity is increasing in leadership and in different industries.

Values are shifting in relationships—less people getting married.

Job performance is measured by results not "time it took to get it done."

The more flexibility you have, the more successful you are.

Clients are fickle and choose brands that they feel aligned with.

Given these changes, how can we elevate the patterns you recognize in your own life and work?

For example, if you work in finance can you see the pattern that clients want more self-serve options, more online options, and more custom solutions?

To elevate this customer behavior pattern in the financial industry, we could look at ways to increase client satisfaction through automating certain services. For example, online mortgage applications that use AI and automation to provide preliminary approval. The opportunity is for a review of how to improve customer care by allocating certain customer interactions to meet the self-serve pattern of financial clients.

Take a look at each of the statistics below and use it to help you look at your life and your work with an eye on predicting the future.

If the human brain is processing enough data to overload a laptop in one week, what does that tell us about the patterns of what people will be seeking?

Patterns of human behavior point to a future where people will be seeking respite from technology, looking for increased entertainment on demand, will want more available programming on streamed outlets, strategies to stay healthy, ideas on how to detox from technology, and much more.

Statistics gives us pattern recognition insights that can help us elevate our thinking, elevate our approach to employees and clients, and elevate our ability to better prepare for the future, rather than be blindsided. Crowdsourcing data through social media, surveys, and AI can provide additional insights into patterns too.

The D in the PREDICT model stands for Directs, which means we can now look at our options for the future. The future is not a single option and it is not predestined. WE create the future, and there are a variety of directions we can go. The future is not a far off concept—it is actually now, and what we do and direct "now" creates the future.

The key in choosing directions for the future is to look at both the technology patterns and the human behavior patterns. In the "directs" part of the process, we look at how we can innovate and create new processes, structures, and systems to help create the future.

This means that strategically when looking at how to ensure future success, we start with this innovation question:

How can we create the best client innovation that solves a need?

Asking "people-first," value-focused questions ensures that we are creating a future that is focused on improving solutions for humans rather than thinking first about profits or the technology.

Another question to ask as it relates to company culture could be:

How can we create a culture where people are treated with the utmost care and are happily engaged with us as a company?

When you think of companies that are very successful today, it is because they started with a focus on people and they continue to focus on adding value and improving lives for people.

An obvious people-focused/first brand is Apple—when the first Apple product was created, the story goes that Steve Jobs wanted to create a computer for the everyday people. In essence, he wanted to democratize computing to help people improve their everyday lives.

Steve Jobs first focused on the vision he had of the future, which was ALL people using technology to create a better world. His first focus was on how to change the world and his technology was the "tools" to help people create and innovate.

Much has been written about Jobs and his creativity, but he admitted that seeing "patterns" in things was the secret to his ability to help bring his vision to fruition. In January 1983, Jobs recalled he had seen the Alto computer developed at Xerox PARC, and he was very excited when he saw it because he knew they could produce a better product at a fraction of the price.

Jobs often quoted Picasso's saying, "Good artists copy, great artists steal." However, ideas are only one part of the equation—the execution is the defining part of successful implantation of an innovative idea.

With every product innovation that Apple has created since the Apple Macintosh, the focus was and has been on how to innovate the user experience. Today we have touch technology on all Apple products, including my MacBook Pro with touch bar that I am writing with right now.

The directs part of the PREDICT acronym is about choosing the innovation of ideas, products, and services with a focus on direction—right now with your life and your work, ask yourself the following:

Given the direction of our industry, patterns in customer behaviors, and what competitors are doing, what are my personal options and what are our options as a company?

Given the pattern recognition and the ability to elevate those patterns to options, think now of the options you could have—let's use the example of a financial professional again.

Option One:

With rapid integration of AI and automation, you could upskill to higher levels of technology skills and shift into the technology side of the business.

Option Two:

You could focus on becoming a generalist in client services rather than specialist and become a virtual client solutions professional.

Option Three:

You could invest in a fintech firm and become an advisor to other financial firms.

Option Four:

You could leave the financial industry and become a contractor for a variety of industries.

Each option requires energy and a desire to direct one's energy toward creating a different future.

If you are a company offering financial solutions, you could have a few options:

Option One: You could invest in technology to have the latest AI, Blockchain, automation, and technology tools for the industry.

Option Two: You could acquire other fintechs who already have the technology and enter into a merger that increases size and scope of client services.

Option Three: You could sell the business and be acquired.

Option Four: You could completely change the trajectory of the business and go into bitcoin as the main focus of the business.

Again, each option requires one major component to be future ready and that is to be able to make the necessary *changes* needed to create the future.

A client we have consulted with for a few years has integrated the PREDICT model into strategy and future success. They are in the insurance industry and took the NextMapping™ "people-first" focus to heart. They created their tagline to explicitly say that they are a "people-first" organization. In doing this they have re-looked at all of their processes, their technology, and their structure with the PREDICT model. They have directed the research and the trends that were identified and took the lead on stating that they were focused on people as the foundation of all of their strategic approaches.

As a result, they are now industry leaders, and their focus on simplifying systems, upgrading technology, and upskilling their employees has helped them to increase both customer and employee happiness. This in turn has increased profitability and made them an industry standout in their "people-first" approach.

Of course, shifting gears and rebuilding the business with a look to the future does not happen overnight—it requires leadership that is willing to change. In addition to the leadership being willing to change, each leader needs to become a master at "leading the changes" needed to create a new future.

Before we get into the changes that have to be made, let's look at the I in the PREDICT acronym, which stands for Investigate.

So far, we have identified that pattern awareness helps to set a starting point for predicting the future. From there we established that pattern recognition is a skill toward being one step ahead for the future. Then we looked at elevating pattern recognition into what we want to create, and lastly, we looked at the choices or direction options we have when creating the future.

Now we look at **Investigating** the best of the past with an eye on creating potential futures.

Investigation is also about checking out ideas, processes, and things that are seemingly different in order to innovate something new.

Continuing on with Jobs and his desire to create something that helped people, Jobs also had unique ideas about how to approach the design process as well as how to run a business.

Just as Jobs was able to gain ideas from the Xerox Parc visit, he was greatly inspired by Edwin H. Land, the inventor of and founder of Polaroid.

Walter Isaacson, in his biography of Steve Jobs, quotes Jobs as saying that Land was one of his childhood heroes. A Polaroid veteran's recent accounts detail the lessons that Jobs took from Dr. Land. These lessons would shape Apple's culture and fuel Jobs's determination to help that culture survive his own death.

Land felt that business was best when it was at the intersection of art and science, and this extended to everything at Polaroid, including product creation, advertising, and corporate culture.

The Polaroid camera has made a resurgence today in the highly technological world of iPhone cameras and Instagram. Why? Because at its essence the Polaroid captures moments and freezes them and instantly shares them in hard copy. The integration of meaning and creativity for customers.

This is a great example of watching the trends in technology and human behavior along with the statistics. It could be predicted that the Polaroid would have a comeback based on buyer nostalgia and whimsy with vintage products that were part of a cultural period.

Land also inspired Jobs to run his company with an ideal balance of managers and dreamers. This too is an investigative approach by merging two seemingly opposite approaches. Most companies have created silos between the managers and dreamers, which limits both innovation and execution ability within a company.

The last investigative learning that Jobs gained from Land was to trust the facts, even if you didn't like them. This is why Apple's rigor around market feedback was integral to the culture. Rather than ignore negative customer feedback, Jobs wanted to investigate, know, and understand the real, hard facts in order to continually improve products for customers.

This is why in the investigate part of the PREDICT acronym the focus is on assessing the past, elevating pattern recognition, and creating choices. In the investigation, we actively look for the "flaws" of the options, the direction, and we use the feedback to help discern the most viable future option for ourselves or for the company.

The ability to seek flaws may seem the opposite of innovation, however Jobs's fixation on looking for problems elevated all product development.

Every team needs people who are good at finding problems and pointing out opportunities for improvement.

The most difficult part of anticipating the future and moving toward creating it is making the *changes* that are necessary to get there.

In my book, *The Art of Change Leadership – Driving Transformation in a Fast-Paced World*, I provide the reasons change is difficult and provide strategies and models to help people and organizations make the needed changes to be successful and future ready.

A lot of the changes that need to be made are difficult because they involve fundamentally changing the culture and people's mindsets.

> *The changes can be small or they can be full transformation, but in order to predict the future you have to be willing to change what's no longer serving the present.*

NextMapping™ is our process for providing the next steps needed to go from where you are now to the future you want to create, whether that is personally or professionally. I will share more about the entire Next-Mapping™ process in parts two and three of this book.

I was the keynote speaker for a conference in Arizona, and the audience members were salon owners in the beauty industry. The focus of the conference was on innovation in an industry that is experiencing multiple disruptions.

Some of the major changes that the industry is going through include specialty franchises taking a piece of the market with services, such as Blo Dry Bar or Dry Bar for example.

Other changes are automated bookings, millennials wanting to freelance rather than work full time in a salon, the "Uberization" of the industry with on-demand services and pop-up shops, and more.

I had conducted a survey of the salon owner audience in advance of my keynotes, and based on their responses and research, I had provided them with three different scenarios with the changes that could be made to be future ready.

The three scenarios I gave them were:

Scenario #1 – To continue to be a traditional organization with brand equity, which means the salon was a long-established brand with traditional structures.

> » Upgrade their technology to include text booking, automated responses to booking, automated reminders, and automated thank you to clients.

> » Upgrade their social media to be more client focused, which would include client video testimonials, comic strips on salon experiences, quizzes, and more.

> » Focus on core business while creating an innovation team within the business.

> » Build teams with "flex" staff to offer flexible work schedules and options.

Scenario #2 – Hybrid strategy of having both a traditional business while concurrently building a mobile or pop-up business arm.

> » Create millennial and Gen Z focus groups for innovative client ideas, hiring ideas, and business ideas.

> » Have a team focus on core business maintenance.

> » Have a team focused on innovation.

> » Create an innovation hub with goals and outcomes for new products and service innovation each month.

> » Have a business unit focused on mobile and pop-up and run it concurrently with traditional revenue sources.

Scenario #3 – Change strategy and transform the business.

» Complete shift on the focus of the business. For example, give up high-cost leased spaces and move to mobile beauty services with less staff and completely supported by AI, automation.

» Create strategic partnerships that support brand and growth, for example Dry Bar and Nordstrom (Dry Bar offers blow dries in store and Nordstrom sells all Dry Bar hair products).

» Create an Uber-like app that matches service providers with customers, with options of going to the customer like a "beauty squad" or customer comes to locations of most convenience.

» Add new value through custom apps, incentives, rewards, and build influencers through satisfied customers to share the brand through social media channels.

» Merge with or acquire "like" or "synergistic" businesses such as other specialty beauty brands or even technology brands like Uber.

As you can see with the scenarios I provided, each requires some level of change. To make incremental change requires energy and commitment and having everyone onboard with the changes. To make massive change, as in scenario #3, requires courage and the PREDICT approach in order to take action aligned with consumer behavior changes as well as realities in the industry.

With the C for Change part of the PREDICT acronym, one of the questions that needs to be asked is:

What changes need to be made in order to create our next level of success and to anticipate further changes in our industry?

The changes needed to be future ready can include:

» Assessing the current leadership mindset—are the leaders focused on creating the future?

» Asking for feedback from employees AND customers and being willing to focus on the cold hard truths of the feedback.

» Looking at the disruptions in technology and your industry to see where you are now in comparison and identifying the gaps.

» Investigating other industries, unlike yours, to seek ideas and opportunities

» Taking action on feedback to create immediate innovations for clients and employee happiness.

» Assessing current legacy systems such as ERPs, CRMs and acknowledging if it's time to let go and update.

» Analyzing current processes, identifying those that are outdated, and updating to meet current client and employee needs.

» Communicating vision to company, providing skills upgrade to leaders and teams, giving resources for employees to be more autonomous.

» Creating a culture of people-first solutions along with creative and innovative thinking that rewards ideas and solutions.

These are just a few of the changes that can be made in anticipation of the future; ultimately what you want is the ability to transform the future to meet change before you are the victim of change.

Which of the above changes have you made personally?

Which of the above changes has your company made?

Which of the above changes does your company need to make?

The T in the PREDICT acronym stands for the Transform of the future—transform is where everything in the PREDICT model comes together.

Transform is where you have a pretty clear picture of what has to transform in order to be future ready.

When you see the patterns, the opportunities and are willing to let go of how things have been or have been done, you are on the right track. You now have a great setup for being on the leading edge of transformation and being the creator of your destiny and the future of your company.

Let's take a look at companies that transformed into completely new versions of their initial businesses.

In 1984, IBM was the leader in the computing world with its PC. IBM was successful because it didn't try to do everything. Unlike Apple, which built its own hardware and wrote every line of software for its computers, IBM bought hardware components from smaller manufacturers and shipped its PCs preloaded with Microsoft Windows.

Ironically, the very strategy that made IBM the darling of Wall Street almost led to its demise. Soon "PC clones" flooded the market, each built with less expensive components and running the same versions of Windows. At that time, IBM was slow to innovate, allowing nimble competitors like Apple to undercut its prices.

The brave decision was made to abandon the core of its business model—building and selling low-margin PCs, computer chips, printers, and other hardware. IBM's new focus would be providing IT expertise and computing services to businesses.

The reinvention of IBM is studied in business schools as a model of corporate transformation.

Using the PREDICT acronym, IBM leadership saw the patterns of the market, recognized the competition was going to continue to compete on price, looked at their core competencies and opportunities, looked at options to direct the business, and ultimately transformed the core business.

As of July 2018, IBM has had its third consecutive quarter of revenue growth following five years of revenue declines. IBM's growth in 2018 included revenue from its strategic focuses of social, mobile, analytics, and cloud.

The company's biggest segment is technology services and cloud platforms, completely different business than what it started out as.

Another company that completely transformed its business model is National Geographic. It started out as a magazine company in 1888 and was a staple in the homes of traditionalists and some baby boomers, but started to lose subscribers in the 90s.

The CEO, John Fahey, had the innate PREDICT approach in his leadership style and, rather than wait for his magazine to suffer the fate of other magazines such as Life magazine, he could see the shifts in how people consumed information. He led the reinvention of National Geographic from magazine to multimedia platforms, specifically the National Geographic Channel. Rather than nature documentary shows, The National Geographic TV programming focused on reality series, such as "Border Wars" and "Ultimate Survival Alaska," and today's programs include "Genius—The Story of Picasso" and "One Strange Rock" with Will Smith.

National Geographic leadership had innovative help from Rupert Murdoch to reinvent and also have great success with their social networking and photo sharing sites, which have given them a whole new way of showcasing the award-winning photography they have been known for.

National Geographic has invested in some high-profile strategic partnerships too, most recently in 2019 with Prince Harry, who shared photos of trees in Malawi on Instagram in partnership with National Geographic.

Personal transformations are part of being future ready. When you think of someone who completely changed the direction of his or her life what was it that caused them to transform?

For many people, they wait until a major life event happens before they make a big life transformation—this could be divorce, death, loss of a job, or any other major life disruption.

One of the reasons I am so passionate about helping leaders, teams, and entrepreneurs to be future ready is that I would like to see people make transformations BEFORE waiting for a big life event to force the change.

It is extremely inspiring to see people who have transformed their lives through circumstances and make changes that shift the entire trajectory of their lives.

How about the story of <u>Brandon Stanton,</u> a photographer and creator of Humans of New York, an online photography project that's become a global phenomenon, propelling him onto the list of Time Magazine's "30 Under 30 People Changing the World." But he wasn't always so creatively focused; he started out in finance as a bonds trader.

His well-thought-out plan was to make money first, save it, and perhaps do something artistic later in life. But he was so unhappy in his finance job that didn't fulfill him. Eventually, he lost his job, and it was the wakeup call he needed to make a career direction change. Stanton, with zero photographer's experience, was inspired to pick up a camera, start shooting and interviewing passers-by on the streets of New York, then posting on Facebook. His work quickly went viral, and today, the blog has more than 17 million followers on Facebook, has led to a best-selling book, and is hugely influential around the world.

In the workplace, we need to be able to provide opportunities for employees to transform themselves through their work, to seek their dreams and help them do what it is they love.

What are some ways you could transform yourself?

What in your wildest dreams would you be doing, other than what you are doing now?

What changes would you have to make to transform?

As an organization, are you transforming at the speed of change?

As an organization, are you providing opportunities for your employees to transform their lives?

https://nextmapping.com/nextmapping-infographics-download/

Working through the PREDICT acronym provides a great foundation for individuals or companies to anticipate the future of work.

Check out this infographic on the PREDICT acronym, and check out the resource list in the back of this book to download all of the infographics presented in this book.

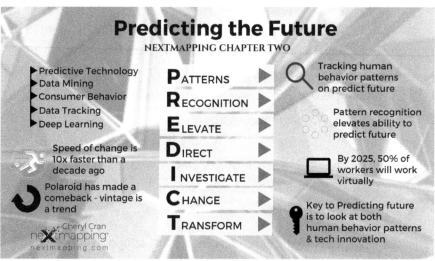

Now that you have some sense of how you could anticipate the future, let's move into part two, where we will focus on "navigating" the future of work.

PART TWO

NAVIGATE THE FUTURE OF WORK

CHAPTER THREE

THE MINDSET OF A NAVIGATOR OF THE FUTURE OF WORK

"The future lies before you like paths of pure white snow.
Be careful how you tread it, for every step will show."
Author Unknown

Do you remember when we used paper maps? Then MapQuest and then GPS. Can you remember (if you are old enough) how you would navigate?

I have a vivid memory from fifteen years ago of travelling all over North America when I was a contract trainer for a seminar group. I was a contracted leadership trainer at the time, travelling by plane and rental car to my events. One memory stands out as I was driving on a dark road and had to pull over to turn on my overhead light and try to decipher the map. It was a lot of added stress to get to the next location and having to navigate to get there.

The creation of MapQuest helped because then I could print off the directions, but in the early days of MapQuest, the routes weren't always accurate, and so that was difficult to navigate as well. And I still printed off the MapQuest directions and had to read them with my overhead light on. Everything changed with GPS, which was mounted to the dash, and then I had a personal navigator to help me (still not perfect). Today's innovation is we use Google Maps on our mobile devices (or built into our vehicles) to help us navigate to where we walk, bike, or drive.

Today we have Uber and Lyft to drive us, and they use Google Maps on their devices. I no longer have the stress of figuring out how to get to my clients' locations. In 2020 we will have more progress with autonomous vehicles, and very soon we will be in driverless cars navigating routes to help us get around.

Now, if only we could have virtual navigators that could navigate the future for us!

Although having a virtual crystal ball could be a future invention, until then we have to work with what we have—our minds.

To navigate the future of work, we need to start with programming our mindsets.

Think of your brain as Google Maps and your thoughts are the routes.

A few questions for you to consider:

Do you have a "futurist mindset," which means you are working in the present while consistently anticipating the future?

Do you have a "change leader" mindset that inspires others to join you in creating the future?

Does your team have an optimistic and abundant mindset about the future?

To successfully navigate the future, you first have to lead yourself, and there are three mindsets that leaders, teams, and entrepreneurs need to develop. They are:

1. The abundant future mindset

2. Creative solutions mindset

3. People-first mindset

THE ABUNDANT FUTURE MINDSET

In his book, ***Abundance: The Future Is Better Than You Think,*** Dr. Peter Diamandis provides scientific research and proof that the world is actually doing better than is reported. Diamandis posits that exponential technologies and groups of people with compelling "moonshots" are making the world a better place, and rapidly.

In his book, Dr. Diamandis identifies how progress in technology is leading us to an abundant future.

He goes on to say that progress in artificial intelligence, robotics, and many other technologies will enable us to make greater gains in the next two decades than we have in the previous two hundred years.

We will soon have the ability to meet and exceed the basic needs of every man, woman, and child on the planet. The book provides a realistic and optimistic view that abundance for all is within our grasp.

In a report by late Swedish academic Hans Rosling, he found something quite interesting. What he found was that very few people in advanced economies know that the world is actually becoming a better place. In fact, he found that many people mistakenly believe the opposite to be true. The news and media focus on reporting wars, famines, catastrophes, and terrorist attacks.

Positive facts, such as the fact that every day some 200,000 people around the world are lifted above the two dollar a day poverty line. Or that more than 300,000 people a day are gaining access to electricity and clean water. Stories of progress in low-income countries just don't get the coverage. Rosling pointed out in his book *Factfulness* that focusing on bad news causes people to become apathetic about the future.

Globalization has put downward pressure on middle-class wages in advanced economies while at the same time has helped to lift hundreds of millions of people above the global poverty line in regions such as Southeast Asia.

An additional positive shift is the increase of life expectancy. Whereas in the Industrial Revolution the average life span was thirty-five years of age, today the average life expectancy is seventy. Other abundant facts include the increase in global income distribution, fewer wars and conflicts, and more people living in democracies.

Not everyone has an abundant mindset, and often there are those who focus on scarcity rather than abundance and pessimism rather than optimism. People who focus on scarcity and pessimism are looking at reality through a "fear" lens. They are looking for "proof" that the world is in bad shape versus looking for proof that things are improving.

To successfully navigate the future of work, we must be pragmatically optimistic with an abundant lens.

Scarcity mindset is at its foundation fear based—fear of not enough for self, fear of not enough for family, and fear of losing out on opportunities. If we refer back to Maslow's hierarchy, scarcity is the mindset of basic survival. The behavior of protecting what you have at all costs, which leads to protectionism, isolation, and stasis.

Think of a time when you were uncertain about a change or your life was disrupted in some way. Did you feel the fear and then seek an abundant focus? If you were fearful for a long period of time, what were your fears based on? Were you able to see beyond the fear to positive facts and actions?

An abundant mindset focuses on the facts while holding a positive view of potential futures, uses tools such as PREDICT to see what possible futures could be created, and inspires others to join in creating a better future.

To provide further context on mindset, check out the short explanation from Carol Dweck (and her popular book *Mindset: The New Psychology of Success*), who states:

"We have a belief which limits our potential or enables our success. It often marks the difference between excellence and mediocrity. It influences our self-awareness, our self-esteem, our creativity, our ability to face challenges, our resilience to setbacks, our levels of depression, and our tendency to stereotype, among other things. Much of who you are on a day-to-day basis comes from your mindset. *Your mindset is the view you have of your qualities and characteristics—where they come from and whether they can* change."

> **Whether you are a leader, a team member, or an entrepreneur, your success is directly related to your mindset.**

Let's look at the mindset differences between scarcity and abundance:

Scarcity Mindset	**Abundance Mindset**
Negative	Positive
Play it safe	Take a risk
There is not enough	There is plenty for everyone
Protect for self	Share with others
Lack in life	Multiple opportunities
Fearful	Courageous
Focused on "me"	Focused on "we"

People who live from the scarcity mindset struggle with self-esteem, have less creativity, and see their struggles as being caused by outside forces. A common behavior of those who are predominantly focused on scarcity is to blame, shame, and find fault with others and self rather than take responsibility for self.

Conversely, people who live from an abundant mindset have high resilience, use creative solutions to solve problems, have high self-belief, are more likely to share, and see their lives as a creation of their own thoughts, behaviors, and actions. People with an abundant mindset inspire others due to high self-esteem, high self-value, and value others too.

Think of some well-known entrepreneurs, people like Elon Musk, Richard Branson, Oprah, Sheryl Sandberg. . . . And we can identify the mindset that got them to their current successes. Having an abundant mindset as it relates to the future does not mean that we ignore reality or that we won't suffer hardship. On the contrary, life still happens! What an abundant mindset provides is positive focus on the future with confidence in our personal abilities that we can direct our future.

Elon Musk has a strong abundance mindset, looking to the future of more electric cars than fuel-filled cars. The company Tesla has struggled and currently is going through a challenge, and ultimately it is Musk's inherent belief in what they are creating and its impact on the world that keeps him driving forward with Tesla. The struggles do not deter the determination of the future—they are merely opportunities to seek an abundant solution to create the future.

Richard Branson of Virgin Group has an abundant future mindset—he holds the vision of the world being a better place and of connecting the world, whether that be through travel or mobile, and his abundant vision is about "connection." Sheryl Sandberg, COO of Facebook, has an abundant mindset about the future of Facebook and, with the privacy and hacking setbacks, continues to hold the vision that Facebook can solve the data breach challenges and still be a force for good in connecting the globe. On a personal level, she suffered the loss of her husband and has turned that into a way of giving back and helping other women stay abundantly minded, even through hardships.

Oprah talks openly about her life hardships and how, even in her darkest hours, she was able to keep an abundant-focused mindset on her future and how she could create a positive and meaningful future despite the challenges she faced in her life.

Inevitably if your mindset is primarily abundance focused, you will find that your life follows your primary thoughts. You are able to stay positive, to stay confident in your abilities, to trust that an abundant outcome is ahead, and generally you are a role model to others in living with an abundant mentality.

Identify when your thoughts are veering toward scarcity—how do you behave when you believe that things are negative or scarce?

Do you tend to focus on what's wrong with a person or situation?

Do you tend to blame others or situations rather than seek solutions?

The key behaviors associated with a scarcity mentality include being judgmental, competitive in an unhealthy way, aggressive, guarded, and trying to keep others from impeding your personal success.

Identify when your thoughts are focused on abundance and an abundant future—how do you behave when you believe things are positive and abundant?

Do you tend to focus on what's right with a person or situation?

Do you tend to seek to understand and find patterns that lead to creative solutions for you and others?

When we have an abundance mentality, we are open, we are generous, we are creative, we share ideas and resources, and we help others succeed and grow.

The point here is not to create polarity between scarcity and abundance, rather the goal is to create greater awareness of the mindsets so that we can consciously choose the mindset that is going to support our goals in creating the future. Of course, we are human beings so we will vacillate between fear and abundant thoughts throughout the many situations we face in a day. By becoming aware of the differences between fear-based thinking and abundant thinking, we can become more alert to when our mind is wandering into fear-based territory. Once we become aware, we can reframe our thinking toward abundant thoughts. The ability to reframe quickly is an adaptability skill that is much needed during these uncertain times.

Abundant-minded leaders of companies such as Uber, Lyft, and Airbnb created from a "share" mindset, which is a component of abundance mindset. Uber was created as a technology company that uses technology for riders to "shares rides." I use Uber when I travel, and I have talked with many Uber drivers who have shared how driving for Uber has paid for their schooling or helps them get out of the house post retirement or has given them an opportunity to work when they want to work.

Notwithstanding the corporate struggles that Uber has faced, the service itself is an abundant mentality service. The thinking behind the Uber service is:

- » Provide ride options to people to get from A to B.
- » Provide car-sharing options for people.
- » Provide fewer cars on the road and, therefore, better for the environment.
- » Provide part-time or full-time work for the drivers.
- » Provide convenience to people through its latest "Uber Eats" service.
- » Provide safety and protection while in cars

Airbnb is another example of a "share or abundant" mentality as it relates to providing places for people to stay. Airbnb was created as a way to share spaces and provide for people to have more options when travelling. Airbnb also provides value to users of the service by giving the experience of "living like a local" in the cities it serves.

There are still some regulatory stuff being sorted regarding Airbnb, and with that we can still see the abundant thinking behind Airbnb:

» Provides places to stay that give people a "stay like a local" experience.

» Provides ways for people from all over the world to connect.

» Provides meaningful experiences for travelers.

» Provides revenue for Airbnb hosts.

» Provides revenue for the cities that have regulated the stays.

» Prevents environmental waste by having less "empty homes."

I know of an Airbnb host who has praised the service for allowing her to be able to pay off her mortgage quicker and others who have said they have met friends for life through the service.

As a leader, an abundant mindset means that you would have the following thoughts about yourself:

1. I am confident in my abilities.

2. I trust that I will make the right decisions.

3. I am positive that I have what it takes to succeed.

4. I believe I am in the right place at the right time.

5. I know I am responsible for the future that I create.

As a leader, an abundant mindset means you would have the following thoughts about others:

1. I have confidence in my team.

2. I believe every person on my team wants to succeed.

3. I am willing to share what I know with my team.

4. I am willing to consistently help people grow.

5. I know that my leadership sets the tone for my team's performance.

As a leader with an abundant mindset, you would have the following thoughts about the future:

1. I am excited about the future.

2. The world is improving—things are improving overall.

3. I am willing to work together to create a better future.

4. I trust I/we can handle what the future brings.

5. Bring on the future—we got this!

THE NEXT MINDSET NEEDED TO BE AN INSPIRATIONAL NAVIGATOR OF THE FUTURE IS THE CREATIVE SOLUTIONS MINDSET.

You likely already have a creative mindset in your life AND the opportunity is to increase our focus toward ongoing and consistent real-time creative solutions in our daily work.

Creative solutions can often come from everyday situations and are a result of cortical collisions, which are two things that seem to be different but that actually have something in common. Thinking back to Jobs and his visit to Xerox PARC, he saw the computer and its components, compared it to the LISA that they were working on, and was able to make the connection to what needed to change in order to make a superior computer.

If you think of some of the inventions we use every day, they were created as a result of a cortical collision—think of:

Duct tape - originally invented by Johnson & Johnson's Permacel division during WWII for the military. The military specifically needed a waterproof tape that could be used to keep moisture out of ammunition cases.

Soldiers began noticing (cortical collision) it wasn't just good for waterproofing ammunition casings but also worked great for repairing things. They began using it for repairing jeeps, guns, and aircraft. Due to its waterproof nature, strength, and built-in adhesive, they even began using it as a temporary means to close up wounds in emergencies; this is fitting because the closest predecessor of duct tape was also a Johnson & Johnson product used as medical tape.

Sticky notes - in 1968, Dr. Spencer Silver, a chemist at 3M Company, invented a unique, low-tack adhesive that would stick to things but also could be repositioned multiple times. He was trying to invent a super-strong adhesive, but he came up with a weak one instead. This could be used on paper, and thus, the sticky note was created.

iPhone - Jobs was invested in the iPod as their big product in 2007 but predicted that the cellphone competition could hinder the progress of iPod. He put his team onto the task of creating an Apple phone—the first iterations were basically an iPod with phone functions (cortical collision). Jobs wasn't happy with the product and ordered the designers back to the table, who then created the edgeless screen that is synonymous with the iPhone we know and love today.

Take a look at the everyday conveniences that you use, whether it be technology or otherwise, and think about how it was created—take it a step further and investigate how that product came to be. You will find that ultimately it was a cortical collision—ideas overlapping that led to the creation of the new product or service.

If you think of Instagram, it is the cortical collision of a social platform that shares photos, two things that most people love to do. It is a unique platform, different than Facebook, Twitter, or LinkedIn, and has its unique place in the market.

Creative solutions mindset in everyday life requires discipline—it means that, along with an abundant mindset, you are focused on finding creative solutions, not fault with situations and people.

There are many ways to leverage creativity in the workplace—focusing on creative exercises every week is a great way to keep yourself and your teams focused on creative solutions.

A great book on creativity that has been around for a long time and that I still refer to is *How to Think Like Leonardo DaVinci* by Michael J Gelb—I love the way Gelb positions creativity as a muscle that we must exercise daily, and it's more relevant today than ever before.

Our research shows that robots and AI will be able to do creative heavy lifting, such as do instant "cortical collisions" computations as well as provide pattern analysis in the next few years. Technology will be useful for practical and logical problems, but when it comes to human-to-human creativity WE need to master our creative solutions mindset.

Think about the last time you were irritated with someone at work—typically when we are irritated we focus on how "different" the other person is from ourselves. We get worked up about how he or she "should" do this or "should" do that. Remember that no one likes to be "should" on. Even worse is when we "should" on ourselves.

In reality, we need to leverage creative mindsets to look beyond the differences and instead focus on what we have in common. Once we have identified what is 'in common' we can look to create a new solution.

I am still learning to master this one in that when I get frustrated with someone, I can get short tempered and condescending. I am aware that this is a tendency for me so I practice staying in abundant and creative mindsets. The other day I was frustrated with someone on my team—I didn't feel he was doing what I asked him to do.

I found myself going into comparison, thinking with thoughts such as, "If I did that it would be done by now," or "It's faster if I just do it myself." I caught myself, reframed, and said to myself, "What do we have in common?"

I made the list of what we had in common, which included:

We both care about the business

We both want to have autonomy

We both are successful in our own right

We both bring value to the team

When I shifted into what we had in common, I could feel myself calm down. I gave it a day and then I went back to my team member and suggested some ideas for how we could handle the scenario in the future. He shared his ideas too, and we were able to come to an agreement of the best way to move forward with him taking responsibility for the request.

Some great exercises to stimulate a creative mindset include:

Come up with ten uses for a robot

Come up with ten ways to use a blow dryer

Or think of items you use in your business and brainstorm other uses—for example, if you are in the home-building industry: ten ways to use a nail gun.

The point is that a creative mindset is a crucial future of work skill that is needed by everyone in the company. It is fairly easy to be creative when you are in an abundant mindset and not so easy when you or your team is in a scarcity mindset.

Creative solutions are the only way we will successfully navigate the future; it won't be to use the approaches that have been used in the past.

Let's do a quick checklist of creative solutions mindset and give yourself a check for each element:

Creative Mindset Checklist:

» Consistently keeps an open mind about people and situations.

» Looks for ways each day to creatively solve problems.

» Finds commonality between things that seem very different.

» Daydreams daily about wacky and weird ideas.

» Chooses to see problems as a way to become more creative.

» Reframes problems into creative opportunities.

» Engages team members in brainstorming creative solutions.

» Listens to and reads about highly creative people.

» High self-belief that you are highly creative.

» Uses creativity to increase levels of adaptability and flexibility.

If you checked all ten items, then you are operating with high levels of optimism and creativity on a daily basis. Your team members are energized by your approach, as you are able to help quickly solve challenges between team members as well as for clients. Because you are creative, you are able to "bounce back" from setbacks quickly and see the opportunity from the setbacks.

No matter the amount you checked off, identify the ones you didn't. Those are your areas for development. For me, even though I have been researching, teaching, and leading for over twenty years, I can have moments of forgetting what I know and trouble practicing what I know. The areas of creative mindset where I can struggle is with reframing problems into creative opportunities in a timely way. I will get there eventually and am highly aware that this is an area where I can get stuck. I can also do better at engaging team members in creative solutions because I can get stuck in the belief that I have to figure it out by myself.

The point is to navigate the future and create the future that you want that will benefit others and ultimately the world. We need to build our mindsets to be abundant and creative.

Some of the innovations in the past ten years could not have even been imagined and yet, through creative mindset, amazing things are being and will continue to be created:

Self-driving cars - Google's driverless car project started in 2008, and they have already started testing them in certain US cities. In twenty years or so, they will become the norm. Interestingly enough, the "creative idea" of self-driving cars dates back to the World Fair in 1939 and the concept has been built upon since then. Like many creative ideas, the timing and the funding wasn't right until now for self-driving cars to become a reality.

However, the idea generated all sorts of innovation in the car industry and provoked insights into the future of innovation.

iPad - Jobs went to dinner with a Microsoft employee who bragged incessantly about a new tablet they had in production. It irritated Jobs so much that he decided to take up the challenge for Apple to create the "best tablet ever."

Kickstarter - opened its online doors on April 28, 2009, and sites like Indiegogo, GoFundMe, and Patreon followed it. They changed the idea of funding forever.

AR (Augmented Reality) - In 2014, Google introduced Google Glass—the first augmented reality project. Since then, they have been working on developing the glasses. Augmented Reality is set to be used in many creative ways, such as training and development, more simulation applications beyond aviation and aerospace, and more.

You do not have to create the next big "thing." In fact, the opportunity is to leverage the new creations for use within our lives and work. Also, we do not need to be attached to an idea or brainstorm to being implemented right away. When driverless cars were first conceived, the person, who brought up the idea knew it was a far-off future reality, but that didn't stop the idea from being generated and shared, and ultimately the idea created a "legacy."

Every day we need to ask questions that stimulate creative idea generation, for example:

How could self-driving cars change your industry or your job?

How could the iPad be leveraged in your job or industry, or how are you leveraging it?

How could you create a company "Kickstarter"-like project to raise funds for employee side projects?

How could you use AR in your life or work to learn, practice, or develop new communication or work skills?

How could you use VR in your life and work to "practice" things such as communication, conflict resolution, how to use a technology, etc.?

The creative mindset is one that needs to be nurtured, focused on daily, and shared with others to help us navigate the future that we are creating.

THE NEXT MINDSET THAT NEEDS TO BE ENHANCED IS THE "PEOPLE-FIRST" MINDSET.

As much as technology is innovating reality, there is a risk that we can have reverence for technology over people. We may place more value on what tech can do and how we use it, rather than on the actual human reality of people.

Many view their smartphones as "appendages" and would rather be without food for a day than their technology!

When looking at the many advantages that technology has brought, there are some challenges that have been created as it relates to "connection to people."

Technology Pros	Technology Cons
Online access /speed has increased knowledge	People are overwhelmed
Social platforms have increased sharing	People are abusing platforms
GPS and Google Maps identifies location	People are losing privacy
Allows people to work anywhere/anytime	People are burning out
Provides abundant access to information	People are confused

I am sure you could add to both lists—the point is that for every technology innovation there has been an impact on people. In order to navigate the future of work in a world-changing way, then we MUST have a "people-first" mindset.

This means we need to look first at the potential impact of a technology on people and focus on how the technology innovation will make life and work better for people.

Earlier in this book, I shared the story of the IT leader who was intent on launching a brand-new technology throughout the company without involving her stakeholders or before talking with other departments or asking for feedback.

The story of that IT leader is an example of being focused on the "technology" first and what it can do, rather than on how will people use this, how will it affect the jobs of the people in each department, and how this will make things better for the client.

For the past few years, the focus has definitely been on getting leaders and teams to integrate new and updated technologies. However, by focusing on technology over people first, often the technology roll out did not succeed the way it could have.

Having a "people-first" mindset means that your predominant thoughts are:

» Our teams are highly valuable and we need to engage them in all we do.

» Our clients are the reason we exist; we need to ensure we are adding value.

» My team leader/boss is a person and he/she has goals/feelings/objectives.

» My teammates are people and they have feelings/emotions/goals.

» As a culture, we are focused on helping people succeed.

The questions that we ask when we have a "people-first" mindset include:

How would each department be impacted by this change/technology/direction?

What would be the impact on each person's job with this change/technology/direction?

How does this change/technology/direction make things easier/better for our clients?

What is the best timing of implementing this change/technology for EACH department?

What does each person need in order to fully get on board with this change/technology?

How can we make it easy for people to use the technology in a way that positively impacts his or her actual work?

The actions we take when having a "people-first" mindset would consist of:

» We engage people in creative ideas, abundant focus, by asking for input in various ways: surveys, quizzes, meetings, virtual meetings, and through intranet.

» We welcome questions and clarifications needed by the leaders and teams.

» We take the time to talk to people one-on-one (in person and/or virtually) to engage them in the changes/new technology/new direction.

» We openly share the concerns brought up.

» We poll stakeholders identify "majority" thinking around the changes/new technology/direction.

» We identify our "influencers" and engage them to help us keep people on track with the changes/new technology/direction.

» We regularly update on progress, timelines, and successes.

» We communicate the setbacks and invite ideas on how to overcome those setbacks.

» We reward the teams and celebrate the achievements in a big way and through all communication channels.

» We strive to see challenges from multiple people perspectives—for example through the eyes of different departments, through the eyes of different personalities, through the eyes of different cultures, etc.

When you think of any big change to lead us forward, the biggest challenge is getting people on board as a collective. The likelihood of faster innovation, faster change, and faster progress rises exponentially when we focus on the "people first."

A great example of a company I mentioned earlier that had a "fail," due to focusing on technology first and people second is <u>Uber.</u>

At its core, Uber was created as a technology company—an app-based service that found a niche in the market for ride sharing. The buyer is human and a person, but Uber never really focused on "people first" as its guiding principle.

The focus on technology as a service for Uber meant that the leadership was more focused on profit and expansion rather than on the people who work for them and for the people who use their service.

At the corporate level, Uber had been struggling with its top-level leadership—the well-known stories of chauvinism, sexual harassment, and treating employees badly brought unwanted attention to Uber as a company.

I am guessing that Uber did ask the question of how we can ensure we provide great ride option for people. AND I would also guess that they didn't ask at the beginning how Uber would treat the people who work for them both at the corporate office and as drivers.

In an effort to repair and reinvent its company culture, Uber hired a Harvard Professor, Frances Frei, and her official title at Uber is SVP of Leadership and Strategy.

When asked what Uber did wrong, Frei pointed out three "fails":

1. Uber's senior leaders operated in silos and only had one-on-one relationships with Kalanick, the CEO at the time.

2. The level below the senior leaders consisted of 3,000 managers, and they had rarely had any formal training and most were first-time managers.

3. Uber's leadership and culture was closed and left the 15,000 employees with no understanding of the business strategy.

All of the above fails are about PEOPLE.

Frei's solutions have put Uber back on track and they include PEOPLE-first leveraging technology to help them.

Under Frei's leadership, Uber University has been created. To overcome the typical online training challenge, Frei drew on her experience at Harvard to create a unique learning format that could be scaled to train many people at once. At Harvard, they had used a studio, HBX Live, where a professor stands to deliver the lessons and in front of the professor is a wall of sixty screens (sixty students). This solution was about providing the best way for teams at Uber to learn quickly, stay engaged, and be accountable to the learnings. It's a virtual learning solution (technology) that focuses on people first by having students in a class to be called upon and interact as if in person at a real lecture.

Also, rather than record the lectures and rely on people to access the information at a later date, Uber University created a feature where bystanders could watch the class as an observer "off the wall" and still be a part of the classroom dynamic.

The classes Uber University has offered are focused on "essential human skills" and included topics such as: Build and Rebuild Trust, Leadership Lessons from Rome, and more.

The success of the program has surprised Frei in that over a third of participants were voluntarily asking questions and engaged. Over 6,000 people went through the programs in the first sixty days of launch, which is a pretty big feat.

My guess is as Uber transforms its culture toward "people first," we will see some great innovations and shifts in the business. I, for one, will continue to keep watching to see the cultural changes.

Conversely a great example of a company whose foundation of success was built on "people first" is Lyft.

Here are three specific ways Lyft has succeeded by focusing on "people first."

1. **Lyft has always focused on treating people well.** "The one thing that really sets Lyft apart is how we think about treating people," says Gina Ma, one of Lyft's first employees, who now heads up the company's brand strategy. The reason this is a winning approach is that when a company focuses on "people first," the people will respond by supporting the brand. Lyft maintains that during the Uber scandals they did not do anything new; they simply behaved as they have always behaved, but people are noticing now.

2. **Lyft knows that reputation always impacts people's decisions.** Consumers today want to deal with and interact with brands that make them feel good. Of course, Uber is convenient and is the bigger name in the rideshare industry AND its missteps have caused a "feeling" among consumers that the brand is not as trustworthy as once thought. For example, women riders may choose Lyft over Uber because of the sexism claims against Uber leadership. Or riders may choose Lyft over Uber because tips have always been built into the prices.

3. **Lyft has always been focused on people.** Gina Ma of Lyft says Uber's problems haven't changed Lyft's overarching strategy, but they have given the company more visibility. "People are curious about how Lyft is different and what our value system is," she said. Lyft is small compared to Uber, meaning that it is not in as many

cities as Uber. However, its "people-first" approach has been growing its user base steadily since the Uber revelations have happened.

As we navigate the future of work, I believe we are all being called to be better human beings. This means developing unique human skills that allow us to connect, collaborate, and share among people.

A "people-first" mindset allows leaders, teams, and entrepreneurs to stay focused on the end result, the end user, the end outcome of whatever is created.

The benefits to a company to build a "people-first" culture creates measurable ROI. Studies show that organizations that focus on people first have 41% less absenteeism and 30% stronger customer happiness than other businesses.

The happier the employees, the happier the customers—a client I have worked with, Appirio, operates on this tenet that the worker experience is directly related to the client experience. Some of the research Appirio has done includes:

» Companies with engaged workers see 233% greater engaged clients.

» Companies with engaged workers see 26% increase in annual revenue.

» 70% of companies say that worker experience is important.

» Only 6% of companies invest in "the people/worker" experience.

The happier the people are within a company, the more likely they are to recommend that company to friends as an employer, and happier employees are three times more likely to stay longer.

A people-first mindset by leaders and teams is the baseline for a people-first organization.

Here's a checklist of a people-first "do's" to see how your company is doing:

Does your company ask for input regularly through surveys, quizzes, polling, and through the intranet?

Does your company listen to people about the tools they need to do their jobs better?

Does your company take action on employee and customer feedback to improve processes or services?

Does your top leadership have a "people-first" mindset? Are they accessible? Do they regularly communicate? Do they share vision, mission, and goals in an inspiring way?

Does your company provide training, coaching, and support to help people grow?

Does your company leadership value diverse perspectives and encourage cross-department team projects?

Does your company have flexible work options?

Does your company provide opportunity for growth, learning, and advancement?

Having a people-first mindset means that, in addition to an abundant mindset about the future and a creative mindset about solutions, you have a people-first perspective that allows you to be well rounded in your "future of work" mindset needed to navigate the future.

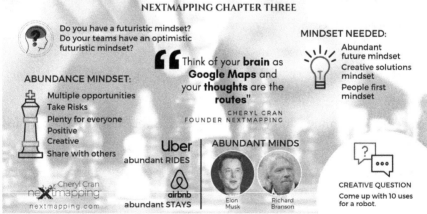

https://nextmapping.com/nextmapping-infographics-download/

CHAPTER FOUR

THE FUTURE IS SHARED (WE)

"Good teams become great ones when each of the members trust each other enough to surrender the me for we."

Phil Jackson

The time for change of how organizations are structured, how organizations share information, and how individuals and teams share success is now!

We cannot wait for the perfect time to initiate the changes needed, nor can we procrastinate creating a culture where people are empowered to advance the vision and mission in potent ways.

We must commit to leading the changes that create a culture where failures are learnings. We must replace attitudes and language of "We already tried that," or "That won't work," with new, creative ideas that are met with the words "Yes, and," as well as "We can make that work."

We have the courage to make change now to create cultures where openness and transparency is the new norm.

We are being called to lead a change in leadership culture, where the predominant words we hear are: "Let's find out how to make this happen," and "Let's focus on creative solutions."

There are two ways to navigate the future; the first starts with "you" as a person and with being able to change our mindsets—we must lead ourselves first (the way we think, create, and share) in order to create abundant individual futures.

The second way to navigate the future is to influence and engage with others. My vision is that as each individual develops his or her best version of self, then together we can create untold breakthroughs and innovations that can truly change the world.

There is research that points to the fact that the future of work will operate more as a "shared leadership" structure than the current hierarchical structures we still see in many businesses today.

Typically, traditional businesses that have been around for long periods of time have grown through the business structure of top-down leadership. In the past, leadership was about a lone or single leader telling team members what to do and how to do it.

Now, and in the future, what it means to be a leader is radically changing. The skills of being a future-ready leader include resiliency, agility, flexibility, collaborative approach, and creativity.

There is a movement toward autonomy and intrapreneurship within organizations. With the increase of remote workers, project work, and contract work, we are going to see even more of a swing toward "personal leadership" where each team member must have foundational leadership skills.

Start-up companies are more likely to structure as less of a top-down leadership culture and more toward team leadership and even co-leadership at all levels within the organization.

There is a need for a new type of leadership for a new and emerging workforce.

Top-down leadership workplaces are no longer the norm.

A *Harvard Business Review* article states that founders who work alongside their teams have the most success. It's becoming more and more common to see founders working alongside interns and teams working together in open space office setups.

The era of cloistered CEOs and senior leadership on the top floor is going away. The co-CEO model has emerged as a result of fast pace of change, increasing need for innovation and no time to waste with siloed departments.

The very term co-CEO indicates cooperation where solo CEOs can be their own silo. Millennials and Gen Z find a collaborative and all-inclusive company culture extremely appealing.

If you are a traditional leader who has come through the decades with a command-and-control type approach, then there is no doubt you will find the very notion of being a co-CEO as a "no go." If you are a "my-way-or-highway" kind of person, you would and will struggle with shared leadership.

Although we could assume that a co-CEO arrangement would be all kumbaya, let's not diminish the reality that there is and would be inevitable conflict. In order to be an effective co-CEO, you would at minimum have to have the three mindsets outlined in Chapter Three.

The actual practice of sharing leadership requires tremendous self-knowledge, willingness to cede power, and a desire to focus on the bigger picture, rather than on self-image or self-power.

Companies that have gone the co-CEO route include one of the most well-known early adopters of the concept—Oracle. The co-CEO's Safra Catz and Mark Hurd have been leading the company together and have modelled how it can work for a large organization.

Salesforce recently announced in August of 2018 that COO Keith Block was being promoted to co-CEO alongside Mark Benioff. Block joined the company in 2013 from Oracle and in his time at Salesforce helped triple revenue and increase stock price.

When Mark Benioff was asked why he promoted and gave Block the title change of co-CEO, Benioff stated that it was important to formalize the relationship between Block and Benioff as the company grows and expands. The co-CEO structure works when you have "codes of conduct" and an agreement to present a unified front to the company, clients, and marketplace.

With careful planning and focused intention, successful co-CEO teams are able to stay unified under all circumstances. Some codes of conduct for co-CEOs include agreeing how to handle disagreements and how to be a united when in front of the teams.

The moment co-CEOs make a decision, that decision needs to be an "us" decision with both leaders having a complete commitment to the direction, whether it results in success or failure.

Co-CEOs is one way to model shared power and the future of work trend toward shared leadership—there are numerous ways that leaders, teams, and entrepreneurs can navigate a shared future.

The evolution toward a shared future is as a result of a cultural shift moving from "me to we."

In my book, *The Art of Change Leadership*, I share information on "me to we" from a few models, including Ken Wilber's AQAL model, which is shorthand for "all, quadrants, all levels, all states, all types, all lines." The model is based on integral theory and the five crucial elements required to create the most comprehensive understanding of evolution and the breadth of human thought and human development.

In my opinion, his work is one of the most comprehensive tools on how to achieve the "self-actualization" levels of Maslow's hierarchy.

Wilber provides insights into the lines of development that each human goes through and ultimately how that is reflected in overall progress for all of us as a human race.

Each color in the model represents "level of thought and cultural development." The colors in the model and the meaning starting from lowest to highest are:

Color	Level	Overview	Where it's Found
Brown	Archaic	Survival, instinct, intuition	War zones
Magenta	Tribal	Superstitious, ritual, customs	Traditional cultures
Red	Warrior	Ego, aggressive, patriarchal	Gangs, militia
Amber	Traditional	Rules, morality, conservative	Religion
Orange	Modernist	Rational, science, achievement	Business
Green	Post Modern	Sensitive, world centric	Environmentalists
Teal	Emergent	IntegralHead/Heart, Flex/Flow	Wellness
Turquoise	Mature Integral	Holistic, conscious evolution	Future of world
Ultra Violet	Post Integral	Transpersonal, oneness	Transcendence

The model of colors can be applied to any system or process and can be used to help guide toward aspirational goals of progress as an individual, family, company, or the world. As each of us ascends and evolves our worldviews, we are able to bring more of a shared perspective and approach to all of our relationships.

With progress through the AQAL model, we actually transcend beyond a level and include all of the gifts, learnings, and value of each level. For example, if your company culture is in the red level, then that means you likely have a high focus on sales, profitability, and aggression to get the job done and base success on results only.

The value, of course, is drive, ambition, and achievement; however, if a company stays in the red line of development, the culture can become siloed, internally competitive, and with high levels of burnout.

The colors associated with a shared leadership culture would be the green, teal, and beyond, while including all of the positive aspects of the preceding colors of green, orange, amber, red, magenta, and brown.

When looking at the progression of each color, you can see that it is a model for shifting from "me" to "we."

Often for leaders it can be confusing to make the leap from the reality of leadership today, which requires someone to be in charge, to the concept of "we."

A simple way to think of "me to we" is that we are becoming more interdependent with each other rather than solely independent or co-dependent.

The definition of independent is:

1. Free from outside control; not depending on another's authority.
2. Not depending on another for livelihood or subsistence.

A key component of creating shared leadership, "we," is that the company consists of autonomous and independent "ME's." Leaders commonly feel frustrated or feel like "glorified babysitters" rather than a facilitator of fully-functioning, independent team members.

You cannot create a company culture or teams without independent thinking and behaving individuals.

You have probably heard of "codependency," either through therapy, psychology classes, or through exposure to human behavior studies. The main difference between codependency and interdependency is someone relying on someone else in an unhealthy way, rather than working together in a healthy way.

The definition of codependency is:

Codependency is the concept of a dysfunctional helping relationship, where one person supports or enables another person's addiction, poor mental health, immaturity, irresponsibility, or under-achievement.

You might think that codependency is more of a dynamic in personal relationships, but there can also be codependent patterns in the workplace as well.

An example of codependency in the workplace can be where a leader lets a team member get away with poor performance or supports his or her underachievements. Or a team member knowingly does more work than an underperforming team member because he or she feels bad/sorry for them.

In fact, we can even be codependent on an actual organization in that we may know it's time to move on or to grow, but we stay with an organization anyway because it "pays the bills" or because it's easier than making a change. Often companies that provide "golden handcuffs" are perpetuating a codependent culture. When I was in banking, an example of golden handcuffs included low-interest borrowing and a steady paycheck, which can be viewed as great reasons to work; however, they can also be reasons why someone might never leave. Or stay in unfulfilling work for a long period of time.

The definition of interdependency is:

1. The state of mutual dependence
   a. A form of symbiosis, or close mutual interdependence of two species.
   b. Interdependence of two nations' economies.
   c. Interdependence of mental, physical and spiritual health.
2. A mutually dependent relationship

    d. Interdependence between factors.

Interdependence in a company is a culture where departments share information and resources across the board and are not limited by budget, innovations or resources.

Interdependence between people in a workplace means the sharing of knowledge, ideas, success tips, resources, people, and more to achieve overall goals and objectives.

In a predominantly "me"-minded organization, you have the following cultural phenomena:

- » Large egos
- » Unhealthy competition
- » Throwing people under the bus
- » CYA (cover your ***)
- » Avoiding the elephant in the room
- » Passive aggressive communication
- » Lack of information
- » Silos
- » Punishment by performance review
- » Top-down leadership
- » Lack of autonomy
- » Fear of making decisions
- » Fear of failure
- » Fear of innovation
- » Looking out for self

In a workplace that is moving toward and becoming a "we" organization, you have the following cultural phenomena:

- » Healthy aware egos
- » Healthy competition

- » Helping others succeed

- » Open and honest communication

- » Willingness to address the elephant in the room

- » Assertive communication

- » Abundant open information

- » Transparency

- » Trust

- » Holding each other accountable

- » Interdependence between departments—share all resources

- » Leadership shares power with all levels in company

- » Autonomy

- » Real-time coaching and review to help people learn and grow

- » Willingness to make decisions

- » Willingness to take risks

- » Willingness to fail and learn

- » Willingness to innovate

- » Looking out for self AND others

There are financial gains of moving toward a "we" culture and one of shared leadership.

I want to clarify that with shared leadership, we are creating a mindset and culture shift that then leads to the best structures, systems, and processes for that specific company.

In my book, *The Art of Change Leadership*, I wrote about the movement toward holacracy as one form of a shared leadership model, which companies such as Zappos and GE have been using. Here in this book, I want to provide you with an overview of holacracy and sociacracy to give context and examples of some "shared leadership" models that already exist. My prediction is that companies will create their own versions of "shared leadership" based on cultural and unique dynamics within each company.

HOLACRACY

The question that led to the creation of holacracy included, "What if we lived in a world without hierarchies?"

Brian Robertson, entrepreneur and software engineer, created the holacracy "self-management" system in 2007, and his company, HolacracyOne, and more than 300 businesses worldwide use the holacracy system.

Holacracy provides radical re-thinking of how companies operate by shifting from a top-down leadership model toward a shared leadership model.

The essence of holacracy is to create a flatter organization and to throw out the traditional top-down hierarchical work charts.

Holacracy is structured to be decentralized decision making, which empowers employees and boosts innovation by reducing red tape. In a holacratic system, the company structure focuses on roles or team function, not on power or titles (such as manager or CEO).

The roles consist of responsibilities and are constantly redesigned. The managers are titled "lead links" and do not control people but rather the responsibilities of each role.

Under the holacratic model, each employee fills multiple roles, and teams locally make decisions. At its highest ideal, the company resembles a thriving hub of self-directed, highly innovative teams.

The main promise of holacracy is flat company management with increased cooperation. Advocates for holacracy claim that the structure creates more collaboration between groups that would normally be siloed and therefore leads to increased creativity.

Tony Hsieh, CEO of Zappos, continues to be a proponent of the system. However, there has been some pushback from other companies claiming that holacracy is not a "people-first" solution.

Research by *Gallup Business Journal* found two flaws with the holacracy system. The first is that the holacratic system focuses on process over people. Employee engagement suffers due to focus on adhering to the system and often people and teams can feel undervalued.

Secondly, *Gallup* research has also found that humans have a basic need for clear expectations. The importance of a manager is having a human focused on consistent communication, accountability, and nurturing growth. In holacracy the "lead links" (titles instead of managers) are tasked with *defining* roles and responsibilities, not "leading."

The opportunity for holacracy in the future is to create a greater emphasis on people focus first, not function focus first.

WHAT IS SOCIACRACY?

Sociacracy, also called "dynamic governance," emerged as a management system in the middle of the 20th century.

The key attributes of sociacracy are:

1. Decisions are made by agreement.
2. The organization is structured in circles.
3. The circles are interlinked.
4. The "lead links," formally known as "managers" are elected.

When Brian Robertson created holacracy in 2007, he took the main elements of sociacracy and added a few other elements.

If we were to put holacracy and sociacracy on the "color" scale of the AQAL map by Wilber, the color associated would be teal/turquoise as a "we" construct.

What the two systems of holacracy and sociacracy have in common is that they both enable teams to self-organize. There is no *formal* hierarchy, but rather there is a structure of *functional* hierarchy that focuses on the distribution of power throughout the company.

The difference between holacracy and sociacracy are:

Sociacracy was founded as a social or political ideal with foundational beliefs that the whole world should govern with a "left" political worldview.

Holacracy is not political. It was developed as a way to optimize organizational work flow and to increase innovation and agility.

Sociacracy aims at continuous evolution of a system, however the focus is not on agility. People are not openly encouraged to speak up when they feel something could be changed.

A major goal of holacracy is agility, and people are encouraged to "bring up tension." If something can be improved by changing it, then you are encouraged to speak up.

In the past and somewhat in the present, agility in an organization meant having to convince higher-ups of a recommended change. In holacracy and to some extend sociacracy, that logic is turned upside down. A change goes through once in the circles, which may or may not include input from the senior leadership who put forward the change. The change goes ahead unless a valid argument can be made against the change. By valid this means a logical and clearly defined objection.

In regards to people, sociacracy does not make a difference between people and roles. Holacracy roles are defined, and people are associated with roles. One person can have multiple roles and be a part of multiple circles.

Both sociacracy and holacracy are systems created to "democratize" the workplace and increase collaboration, consensus, and, in the case of holacracy, agility.

When it comes to navigating the future of work, it's vital that we identify the cultural shifts that are required to move toward a "we" or "shared leadership" company.

Research has shown that millennials (23 to 37) and Gen Zs (16 to 22) are attracted to working for organizations that share data, online sharing, resources, and have a shared leadership structure.

The rise of coworking spaces is a great example of a shared future growing rapidly; in the US there will be 3.8 million coworkers by 2020 and 5.1 million by 2022.

Coworking is a great example of a shared leadership way of working.

THE FUTURE OF WORK EVERYONE WILL BE A LEADER

If there is anything that the shared leadership movement is making evident, it's that there will be an increased need for everyone within the company to become more independent and accountable than ever before.

The movement toward independent workers means eventually we will have a whole bunch of entrepreneurs who have developed fundamental leadership and business skills being hired as intrapreneurs within companies.

My definition of an "intrapreneur" is: An independent-minded worker with abundant resources and support to work both independently and interdependently within an organization. The intrapreneurs have the autonomy of being self-employed, along with the built-in team and support of an organization.

Of the next 27 million independent workers, 42% will be millennials. The next wave of independent workers will also be more ethnically diverse then the existing self-employed individuals. The 27 million new independent workers will consist of a higher percentage of African American, Asian, and Hispanic workers.

71% of self-employed/independent workers report having overall high career satisfaction compared to 61% of traditionally employed workers.

The trends toward remote work, independent work, and shared work means that we have to be navigating the new structures for leadership, workplace, and client delivery.

It's not difficult to see that the statement that everyone will be a leader is not a far-off prediction; in fact it's actually happening due to shifts in worker attitudes and work habits being changed.

In order <u>for everyone to truly be a leader, it requires current training</u> on fundamental leadership skills for team members and next-level future-of-work-skills training for leaders and teams.

At NextMapping™, we help leaders and teams create their own ideal shared leadership model without having to fit into the box or structure of sociacracy or holacracy.

Every organization has its unique culture, quirks, and dynamics; that means a one-size-fits-all approach may not be the solution.

Through our NextMapping™ process, we work with you to identify the best way to build on your current culture and success to create a customized "what's next" strategy.

We build on what you have created to date with new systems, integration of existing or new technology, and, based on a "people-first" approach, the best way to create a culture of self-organizing teams.

Not every organization is willing or able to make a complete shift to a holacracy or sociacracy model. The middle ground is a customized, shared leadership strategy.

The components to the NextMapping™ shared leadership approach include:

» Investigating the current cultural norms.

» Setting a compelling vision for cultural change.

» Asking for input from all stakeholders.

» Assessing the "roadblocks" to shared leadership.

» Creating the "map" toward the changes needed.

» Identifying "change leaders."

» Implementing progressive changes toward cultural goals.

» Measuring and monitoring progress.

» Celebrating and continuous improvement.

https://nextmapping.com/nextmapping-infographics-download/

CHAPTER FIVE

NAVIGATING TODAY'S CHALLENGES – WHAT'S NEXT?

"Shifting your perspective is better than being smart."
Astro Teller X

In the future of work, when I say that "everyone will be a leader," it is not meant to be taken literally. Realistically, how could business possibly be run if we have too many cooks in the kitchen?

A trend that is shaping the future of work is workplace leaders proactively providing all people with fundamental leadership skills and abilities. Future-ready teams will be comprised of people who have developed the fundamentals of being a leader such as conflict management skills, collaboration skills, creativity skills, and more.

The rapid pace of change and innovation requires companies to have more people who have leadership ability to better leverage technology, people who can effectively self-lead remote work, and people who form self-organized teams.

Meanwhile, before we get to *that* future we NEED leaders just like you to be the "change leaders," to actually anticipate, navigate, and create the future of work.

There are a lot of current challenges that need to be sorted, and the biggest opportunity for you as a leader is to be able to have the flexibility to navigate current reality while keeping a focus and a plan toward creating the future.

When I work with clients who hire me as a keynote speaker, I use our NextMapping™ process to ensure I am able to provide a customized and insightful keynote.

One of those steps is to ask for their input and their insights on the future of work and the challenges they are facing. I do this in a few ways; first, I meet with the organizing team by conference call or Zoom and gather information about the company, goals for the conference, goals for my keynote, and some of the company challenges they are facing.

As a follow-up to that call, I send out a survey link to the organizing team who then sends it out to all of the attendees of the conference and my keynote. That survey asks for candid and anonymous input into the challenges being faced by the attendees, along with what they are excited about for the future.

Then, I integrate the information that I gather through the survey into my keynote, and during the keynote, I use polling and texting to engage the audience further in ensuring that the message I am delivering is providing creative insights and solutions to their challenges. The goal for me is to ensure I am operating from full context and that I have as much input as possible from all people involved to ensure my message is relevant and valuable to the group.

As you can imagine, we have gathered a tremendous amount of data as a result of doing the surveys, polling, and texting. We have received thousands of responses from leaders and teams in multiple industries, including technology, healthcare, pharmaceutical, finance, insurance, government, and many more.

Top 4 challenges we have found in our surveys include:

» Finding good people

» Keeping good people

» Millennial and Gen Z impact

» Fast pace of change

These challenges are across the board in multiple industries and in a variety of countries. These challenges are a global phenomenon, and even with technological innovation, the challenges are continuing.

The solutions to the above challenges can range from the tried and true and obvious to completely unique innovations and different ways of thinking about possible solutions.

FINDING GOOD PEOPLE

There is a war for talent, and every client I work with laments the difficulty of finding trained and work-ready talent. A colleague, Bill Meador, who is an educator in Albuquerque, New Mexico, has done extensive research on how the education system can better serve employers to solve this dilemma.

Bill was sharing with me on a recent phone call about some unique solutions that are arising out of the need for work-ready talent. One of those solutions is something called "learnerships"—created in South Africa, a learnership is a paid internship program cooperative between educators/colleges/universities and employers.

The current model of education is not helping employers to have workers who can hit the ground running. Many students are getting degrees and being taught concepts, but not the practical application of skills needed in the workplace.

This means that the education industry is also going through a major transformation of moving away from traditional teaching methods and moving toward curriculums and program delivery that results in work-ready skills for multiple industry employers.

In fact, the search for good people is such a challenge that organizations, such as Google and others, are *getting rid of the requirement for college or university degrees* for certain jobs.

Research by Glassdoor revealed that companies such as EY, Penguin Random House, Costco, Whole Foods, Hilton, Apple, Nordstrom, Home Depot, IBM, and Starbucks no longer *REQUIRE* a college degree to secure candidates for jobs.

The case for not requiring a college degree by applicants is that are many talented people who have experience in multiple industries or jobs but do not have a college or university degree. What the non-college or university degree applicants bring to their potential employer is multi-industry knowledge, on the job experience, and on the job education.

The key to navigating the challenge of finding good people now and into the future is having a brand that has built a great reputation around culture and happy worker experience. There is no point to go through the effort to attract good people if equal or more effort is not put into strategies for engaging and keeping people around for a certain period of time.

The reasons finding good people right now is a problem and will continue to be in the future are the following:

» Technology innovation has made finding a job easier for job seekers than ever before.

» There are more competing recruiting firms scouting for people at the same time.

» Millennials have now been in the workforce for a number of years and typically rotate jobs/careers about every 2-3 years.

» Gen Zs are more interested in project work or in becoming an entrepreneur.

» Baby Boomers are retiring AND are willing to do project work, but not full time.

» Gen X want work that allows for the balancing of life, which includes grown kids along with aging parents.

» Competition is fierce, and in some industries more money is thrown around to entice high-performing talent.

» The war for talent is now global, and other countries are scouting talent from organizations that have invested in people's training and development.

» Traditional cultures are struggling to attract younger workers who want the latest in technology tools, fun culture, and inclusive leadership.

Think about your current team dynamics—what is the average tenure of your team members? Why?

If you have long-tenured people, that can be a good thing and a bad thing—having a team of people who have been there a long time without adding new people can lead to status quo attitudes and a lack of innovation. Conversely, having a team of constantly rotating team members can be difficult to keep things on track and consistently moving forward. There is a balance between having a stable team along with rotating team members.

In the future of work, leaders need to look at finding good people from an entirely different perspective.

In order to find good people, companies need to have a culture where there is freedom of autonomy, flexibility of work schedule, inclusive leaders, and a sense of unified purpose within the organization.

Let's take a look the perspective changes a leader needs to make around finding good people:

Perspective of the Past	Perspective of the Future
Finding a person to fill a 'job'	People to collaborate on 'projects'
Expecting person to stay a long time	Knowing average job time is 3 years
Expecting person to be grateful for job	Being grateful for people you hire
Expecting person to stay engaged	Actively engaging people
Person to fit into the team	Creating an engaging team culture
Expecting person to be patient for promotion	Creating career map potentials
Expecting person to be 'ready to hit the ground'	Setting people up for success
Expecting that you only have to hire randomly	New normal of hiring often
Managing a team that is stable teams	Leading constant changing

As you can see, the mindset shift that needs to happen in order for leaders to navigate the future of finding good people includes being flexible, creative, and "people" focused.

In the future, leaders will not have set teams and set team members; in the future, leaders will be co-leading teams that are constantly changing based on projects, mandates, and innovation priorities.

The fight for new, talented people is intense and across all industries. According to SHRM (Society for Human Resource Management), from 2015 to present has been the most difficult and competitive period for finding people.

These days, I advise executives to treat potential hires as they would their customers. Understand their behavior, know where they are hanging out, and design recruiting strategies based on their interests.

Some ideas for finding highly talented people include:

Be aware of being on the same social media platforms as your competitors and think of more specific locations for the people you seek. SHRM reports that 84% of organizations use social media for recruiting. The common thought might be that if so many companies are using social media it must be working.

Think as If There Is No Box When It Comes to Creative Recruiting

Seek out other online platforms rather than relying on social media alone, and look at alternative places for talented people. For example, if you are seeking a part-time worker, post the job on Upwork, Freelancer, or other contract-based sites—you never know that someone may want to commit to a part-time position or add it to their contracts.

Connect with knowledge-sharing online platforms, such as Levo or Millennial Women, a networking site. For people in multiple professions, it might be by Quora. Highfive, a Silicon-Valley-based video and web conference supplier, uses Quora to connect with the type of people they want to attract.

Go to industry-specific online match-making sources, such as fieldengineer.com that matches engineers with opportunities.

Seek out industry associations; for example, if you are seeking technology workers, go to a technology association, such as WIT (Women in Technology).

Take talent recruiting into your own hands. I mentioned learnerships earlier—Genesys is a global customer experience and call center software company. In 2013, they were struggling with delays in bringing on new hires to match the speed of their expansion. The CMO got creative and decided to partner with HR to start an associate program that put new college and experienced professionals together through a three-week training period and pairing them with mentors for ongoing learning.

Attract millennials with humor. GE knew their brand was not synonymous with "changing the world"; their brand was viewed as manufacturing. That's why their ad campaign about Owen, whose parents think his job is just manufacturing went over well with millennials. The ad points out the fact GE DOES change the world, and the ad had an impact on their recruiting efforts aimed at millennials. The "Owen" ad increased job applications at GE by 800%!

You don't need a mega ad budget to do this—with YouTube and social media, as well as placing videos on your website, you can appeal to millennials and Gen Z.

Seventy-seven percent of mobile usage is for video—this means that the more you can communicate the brand of your company, along with compelling video "ads" to attract new people, the more likely you are to increase your number of candidates for those jobs/projects you need to fill. Share video of your engaged, happy employees explaining why they love working for your company and why people should apply to work for your company.

Leverage your existing high-performing people and incentivize recruiting within the organization. Many organizations pay recruiting incentives or rewards in various ways to employees who introduce new hires to the company.

I will be sharing more resources for finding people in the resource section at the back of this book.

The key for navigating the future of work is to be thinking about and proactively planning solutions for the current and future challenges. Finding people is going to continue to be a challenge, as workers seek more project and contract work.

However, if we look at the finding people challenge, through a creative and people-first lens, we can use the shifts as signals for what needs to change now. Often not being able to attract people means there is an opportunity to relook at overall company culture and to make the changes to create a more engaging workplace.

Some questions to consider in regard to the finding-people challenge:

1. If your company has an HR department, are you partnering or co-creating with HR, rather than just expecting them to solve your finding-people problem?

2. Does your culture have a prevalent "filling jobs" mentality, and if so, is there a way you can look at your workplace as a series of projects and therefore hire for dynamic projects rather than jobs?

3. Is your company locked into the "warm body" for a job perspective, and instead, could you be looking at restructuring jobs to suit either a part-time worker or a remote worker?

4. Does your company have a full-time or part-time approach, and are you missing opportunities to hire contractors, entrepreneurs, or freelancers?

5. Do your leaders do a great job of engaging and keeping people happy once they are hired?

6. Is everyone in the company tasked with attracting new workers?

7. Are you looking in creative locations to find new workers? For example, does your industry lend itself to veterans returning from

military duty? Or does your work appeal to working moms who want to work nine to three as well as remotely?

These questions would be great to bring forward to your executive team and your HR team. From there you could create a shared leadership focus for the whole company by creating a survey. Gathering responses to the above questions would provide great context for making change in regards to finding good people.

KEEPING GOOD PEOPLE: A KEY STRATEGY TO NAVIGATING THE FUTURE OF WORK

Even with the rise of remote workers, contract workers, and freelancers, the future of work will still have offices and will still require people in full-time positions for certain roles and functions. The future workplace will consist of a mix of full-time, part-time, contract, freelance, remote, and various global location workers.

In a shared leadership structure, there is still a senior leadership structure. There remains a certain level of layers that are less than a pyramid or typical hierarchy—you still need levels or lines of overseers in order to steer direction within the organizations.

Flatter organizations simply mean "less" levels and, therefore, a company that has the agility of a startup with the leveraging of an established multinational.

This means that now and into the future, we need to hang onto and keep the people who are instrumental in driving business forward and successful.

As I mentioned earlier, if the focus is on simply hiring or finding new people all of the time, there is a tremendous amount of time and money that is going to waste. To successfully navigate the future of work, we need leaders who are able to engage, inspire, and ensure workers are happy and likely to stick around a little longer than the norm.

There is a high cost to high turnover.

A <u>study</u> by the Society for Human Resource Management found that employers would need to spend the equivalent of six to nine months of an employee's salary in order to find and train their replacement.

That means that for an employee salaried at $60,000, it will cost the company anywhere from $30,000 to $45,000 to hire and train a replacement.

In a <u>study</u> conducted by the Center for America Progress, the cost of losing an employee can cost anywhere from 16% of their salary for hourly, unsalaried employees, to 213% of the salary for a highly trained position! ***So, if a high-trained executive is making $120,000 a year, the true loss could be up to $255,600 to the company!***

The factors included in the cost of replacing an employee include:

1. *The cost of interviewing can include time of interviewers, travel, correspondence between decision makers, and mistakes in choosing the wrong hire.*

2. Advertising costs, including social media sites and job sites.

3. Recruiter expenses, which can cost up to 30% of the hired person's salary for senior positions.

4. Onboarding costs, when done properly, can include time to orient new hire, time to introduce to other departments, time to bring up to speed on culture and company dynamics.

5. Training—it takes about three to six months to fully integrate a new hire into the vibe of the company and the team. Both formal and informal training requires a lot of time and resources—today and in the future, this timeline will shrink to hires needing to get on board with all training and readiness within one to two months.

6. If you lose a few good people it can create an "exit" of other people as they see people they admire leave the company. This can result in massive damage, due to loss of more people and more expense to the company.

7. Loss of productivity—there is a decrease in productivity with a new hire as they gain mastery of their role. Josh Bersin of Deloitte claims it's two years for a new hire to reach same productivity level of an existing worker.

8. Impact on morale can result in lost productivity if new hires are not onboarded and integrated into existing culture in a positive and effective way.

9. Customer care can suffer if new hires do not know the answers to frequently asked questions by clients. Issues can take longer to resolve, and business could be affected by lack of product or service knowledge.

So, what are the solutions to keeping good people engaged and onboard?

The key strategies that tend to keep people both engaged and willing to hang around are not surprisingly all about how we treat people. Treating people with care and as human beings is a key component of worker retention.

Professor Rockoff of Columbia University has found that mentoring is a factor in reducing employee turnover, increasing skills of new hires, and increasing productivity of newly onboarded team members.

Professor Rockoff found that students who received mentoring had the best performance and were less likely to drop out of a program. The same is true for business—when an employee receives specialized attention and training from a mentor, they perform better on the job and are more likely to stay longer as well.

Companies like Apple have an average turnover rate of 5 years, Adobe 5.3 years, and Cisco a whopping 7 years.

Interestingly, Uber, who I mentioned earlier in the book, has an average turnover rate of 1.8 years. I think we could directly tie that to the culture issue they have had over the past few years.

Apple, Adobe, and Cisco all have the following elements in common:

Onsite gyms

Discounted products

Allowances for social activities

Mentorships

Project opportunities

Commuter stipends

Sabbaticals

In case you think all technology companies have an advantage over your industry, think again.

Companies like Dropbox struggle to keep people beyond 2 years, Tesla struggles to keep people past 2.1 years, and Square keeps their people 2.3 years on average.

> *Navigating the future of work means we need to look at retention with a creative mindset and leaders need to come to grips with the reality that tenure beyond five years will not be a thing of the future.*

My prediction is that traditional retention strategies will go to the wayside as the workplace continues to change and transform over the next five to ten years.

To be future ready now, I believe leaders need to look at employee "management" and engagement through new eyes and leverage their flexible and creative mindset to come up with new approaches to keep "good people" on board:

» Leaders need to think of ways to engage people each and every day, with a focus on knowing that average time on job is now two years. Leader mindset needs to be ongoing, recruiting and scouting for potential talent.

» Shift mindset to see work as projects and not as jobs, and therefore, look at retention less as a mindset of "keeping someone on the job," and more of a, "How do we keep this person aligned with the company for ongoing opportunities?"

» Leaders need to shift the way they "lead" and think of people as allies and valuable, versus as "solutions to problems" or filling a job.

» In the future, there will be more cross-industry pollination, leaders need to be looking in similar industries for talented people, as well as "out of the box" or unrelated industries that could bring new perspectives and synergy to the business.

» Look at all of your jobs in your company, sit down with your HR team, and literally go through and identify which jobs could be automated, which jobs could be contracted, which jobs are required to be full time in house, which jobs could be filed by remote workers, and imagine a whole new structure to the company.

» Be willing to invest time and energy into grooming, mentoring, and coaching both existing workers with potential as well as new hires that are brought on.

» Accept that job loyalty is shifting, and your new role is to lead in a constantly changing reality with new people dynamics and new rules of the way people want to work.

» Crowdsource your existing teams and find out the average time on job in the company and find out what keeps the long-time workers around.

» Keep "engagement" of your people as a daily top-of-mind activity— think of new and creative ways to say thank you and value your people.

» Create a performance-based culture, not a "long time on job" culture—the days of giving a reward for twenty years on the job are OVER. Instead, recognize and reward those who are driving business forward, innovating, and leading change.

» Be willing to critically self-assess your leadership and have your team assess you critically—ask them if they were in your job what would they do and why. Three hundred and sixty reviews can be highly valuable when administered openly and with open-minded leaders.

» Remember that your competitors for talent in the future may not be other companies but rather the people themselves starting their own startup!

» Through coaching, be willing to help each of your team members succeed, and invest in "good karma"; if you do have an employee who decides to go off and start his or her own business, don't rule them out as a potential contractor or ally.

» Be willing to lead the changes that need to be made to create a culture that is highly engaging for employees. Be creative—you may not be able to provide an onsite gym, but could an influencer in the company lead lunchtime yoga classes?

» Take a look at the list of what the tech companies provide and come up with a creative "work-around" that could work in your company.

» Get creative with *how* work needs to be done—for example, a client of ours had a traditional underwriting job where the worker was struggling with the high-tech aspect of the job. When examining the impact on the business of losing this worker, it was decided to reconfigure the job. This allowed for the company to keep the worker, and it also improved productivity for both the worker and the rest of the team.

When we look at navigating the future of work, we have to consider the impact of millennials and Gen Z.

Forty-six percent of the workplace will consist of millennials by the year 2020.

Millennials (aged 23-37) have been leading many of the changes we are seeing in workplaces and in many cases are the CEOs of many successful tech firms.

As we look at navigating the future as a leader, it's important to see the trends that will be led by Gen Z and millennials combined.

It is estimated that 61 million Gen Zs (people born after 1996) will be entering the work world in a big way starting in 2018. The Gen Z population is larger than Gen X and two thirds the size of Zoomers.

Do not make the mistake of lumping millennials and Gen Zs together. Gen Zs have lived a much different life than their parents and millennials. Gen Zs are a group that want to work hard, learn, and succeed. They have seen their parents struggle financially (due to 2008 recession and student loan debts), and this has caused them to think about creating their own financial future.

When it comes to attracting Gen Zs, they are looking primarily at culture and whether it's a fit. Millennials as well want a fun and growth-oriented culture; together these two generations are going to radically change the world of work both now and into the future.

Both Gen Zs and millennials look to online reviews and peer reviews when investigating companies or brands to either work for or purchase from. Both generations also want fun, flexibility, paid time off, and the opportunity to gain recognition.

There is one criticism that is made about both millennials and Gen Z, which is that they don't know how to have face-to-face conversations or write emails.

You may be interested to know that technology is going to solve that for them. With AI and robots, there will be "coaches" available that with the help of algorithms will be able to help identify the personality of a client or coworker and then guide the user on the right language and the right form of communication to make the most impact.

One complaint of today's generations has been their "writing skills," and AI has come to the rescue. Apps like Grammarly are helping workers to instantly fix grammar and improve writing abilities in real time.

There is a benefit to providing "human skills" training that can guide on human connection skills, such as empathy, emotional awareness, and relationship building.

Millennials have always wanted to have an open and casual workplace where it's okay to ask anyone anything, including senior leadership. Gen Z has the same expectation—they do not see barriers to talking to someone because of title or position.

These two generations want friends, allies, and buddies, and if you are a traditional leader this can cause frustration because of the professional school of leadership, which was all about professional boundaries.

As a leader, you must be willing to give regular and sometimes daily feedback to your Gen Z's and millennials. Forty percent surveyed say they want daily interactions with their boss and need the confirmation that they are doing a good or great job.

Generation Z is <u>55% more likely</u> to want to start a business than millennials. In fact, a full <u>72% of Gen Z high school students</u> say they want to start a business. This can be tied back to many of their traits—especially the independence and desire for financial success. They are highly motivated and willing to work hard to achieve their dreams.

Here are some ways that millennials and Gen Z are influencing the future of work:

Millenials	Gen Z
Increased uptake of technology solutions	Technology WILL lead solutions
Value flexibility and led the remote work	Will seek remote or start own business
Got branded as 'lazy' rather than efficient	Are branding themselves as non- millennials
Expect to be promoted quickly	Will leave if not promoted quickly
Struggling with rules and structures	Will force the remake of rules
Looking to lead in teams	Wiling to lead by self or with teams
Will have up to a dozen of careers	Will have dozens of careers

Millennials and Gen Zs are definitely of the "abundant mindset" about the future of work mentioned earlier—they believe in creativity, people first, and boundless opportunities.

Progressive companies are leveraging the intelligence of their millennial and Gen Z workers by creating "innovation circles" led by these two generations. The innovation circles consist of all ages but are led by millennials and/or Gen Zs.

Tech firms like Google, Twitter, and Salesforce are appealing to the millennials and Gen Zs by having events with rock stars like Bruno Mars playing a concert for the company or other perks that appeal to special experiences.

Therefore, as you look to navigate the future of work, you can see that the challenges outlined in this chapter need to be dealt with today. In addition to the challenges of finding and keeping good people and the impact of millennials and Gen Zs is the additional and ongoing challenge of dealing with the fast pace of change.

FAST PACE OF CHANGE

If you think of a desk and an office ten years ago, here's what we would find:

- » Desktop computer
- » Large hard drive
- » Paper calendar
- » Books/reference books
- » Calculator
- » Stapler
- » Video camera
- » Large cell phone
- » Pager
- » Walkman
- » iPod
- » Polaroid camera
- » Laser dot printer

» Audio recorder

Today, every single one of these items and their functions are now inside a mobile device, laptop, or tablet.

That was only ten years ago. In the next ten years, if we look to 2030, here are the predictions of what we will have:

Self-driving cars

Drone deliveries

Robot assistants

Flying cars

3D printing of everyday essentials including food.

Healthcare breakthroughs resulting in decreased mortality.

Holographic teachers/conferences/events.

Smart cities with automated crime deterrence.

Microchip communication embedded into body.

AI will provide what is needed immediately.

There will be less "ownership" of items and more of a "pay for use" model.

People will be looking for meaningful experiences for themselves and their families.

Work will shift into "purpose," and "jobs" will be replaced with "passion projects."

What else do you think will be a significant change by the time we reach 2030?

The speed with which technology is rapidly changing means it is near impossible to predict what the reality will be in 2030. However, we can keep an eye out for trends and human behavior shifts and begin thinking about how we can leverage the existing technology in current situations.

The reason the fast pace of change is THE biggest challenge for most people is the fast pace of innovation and change, as well as online sharing is creating both panic and anxiety in a lot of people.

The biggest skill that educators can be teaching kids today and that adults need to learn is how to be able to be highly flexible, adaptable, and agile in an ambiguous and uncertain current and future reality.

How do we best navigate the fast pace of change?

The answers are a blend of the esoteric, along with the practical—there has been so much value placed on profits and growth that people are literally burning out. The rate of suicide has jumped dramatically over the past few years, and even more alarming is that young people have the highest rate of suicide.

When in it comes to being flexible, agile, and resilient, we need to be building the internal reserves of strength, faith in self, trust in abilities, belief in ability to adapt, and go beyond the "self" to the unseen.

We are living and working in a time where there is a spiritual void that is causing people to question current reality. The good news is that if we can increase our inner strength, we can follow the calling of the future as a "heroes calling," rather than as a fearful fate.

When I use the word *spiritual,* I am not talking about religion or "woowoo" stuff. I am referring to the reality that there is "energy" that is unseen that can be felt when we are in complete states of relaxation, in nature, or when meditating.

In my book, *The Art of Change Leadership*, I shared a lot about the need to go beyond emotional intelligence and develop a spiritual intelligence.

What I mean by building spiritual intelligence is really being able to self-organize through mindset and activities that allow you to connect to higher amounts of energy and inspiration that goes beyond self.

When we feel empty, alone, or defeated, there is no energy to create the future.

Think of the last time you felt fulfilled, inspired, and connected to more than yourself. When was the last time you felt this way?

Take a few moments to write down why you felt inspired, fulfilled, or connected.

These feelings are key emotions of someone who is spiritually intelligent.

In order to lead yourself and others through the ongoing fast pace of change, you need to spend about 80% of your time feeling inspired, hopeful, and on a mission and the other 20% on uncertainty, doubt, and fear.

Here is a list of the emotions and actions of a spiritually intelligent change leader navigating current and future reality:

Emotions	Actions
Grateful	Shares freely to help others
Inspired	Inspires others with language and actions
Hopeful	Takes risks based on hope for future
Joyful	Use humor and lightness with others
Fulfilled	Takes action aligned with purpose
Passionate	Shares excitement for potential
Awed	Inspired by others
Calm	Trusts in self and in others
Driven	Strong belief in direction
Connected	Wants to make it better for others
Blessed	Sees gifts in good and bad
Humble	Sees wisdom in learning
Purposeful	Wants to be the best version of self

A spiritually intelligent leader/team member has the highest amount of accountability to self, feels a deep responsibility to honor self and others, and sees their purpose on Earth as far greater than being a human being living a physical experience.

In these times of intense pressure and change, everyone is hungry for feeling inspired, for feeling soulful and on purpose, and that hunger is what is driving the creation of the future for all of us.

Each of us is responsible for owning our energy, owning how we impact others, and owning the future we are creating. If you struggle with losing the vision or feeling anxious or afraid of the unknown future, it is an opportunity to take ownership of the resources you need in order to feel your most inspired, most connected, and most trusting of the future.

Here are some ideas for staying energized and spiritually intelligent as you navigate the future of work (and life).

» Learn to meditate, and there are many ways to meditate—there are apps (Calm and Headspace are two examples), online guides, teachers in your community, and more. You can meditate while walking, being in nature, and sitting at your desk or workspace.

» Seek out a coach who has the depth of psychology, along with spiritual intelligence and workplace application. Be accountable to a coach to help you navigate uncertainty and the future.

» Read or listen to inspirational books. I read a chapter from a spiritual book every night before I fall asleep—it inspires me and puts me into a positive sleep state.

» Get out in nature at least twenty minutes a day—take a phone call outside, sit on a park bench, walk near the water. If you can't get outside, then watch a nature video on YouTube (proven technique to calm and center).

» Set up a buddy system with a mentor or someone you can trust who can hold you accountable when you are afraid, negative, or anxious. Text them, call them, or meet them—human-to-human contact is crucial to connection and well-being.

» Trust that you are here on Earth for a purpose. Go to a program or take an online program about aligning with your purpose, your soul, and your passions.

» Build greater self-awareness of when you are being defensive, overly aggressive, pushy, unreasonable, and even childish—vow to be more accountable for your behavior and apologize when you harm someone with your anxious behavior.

» Be brave to ask for help and use the help that is available—if your workplace provides counselling or support, make sure you take advantage of the opportunity.

» Communicate to your own level of comfort your failures and feelings as well as your successes—authentically sharing your process builds deeper connection and camaraderie with your teams.

» Find ways to nourish your spirit/soul—what brings you joy? For me, if I listen to mantras or gospel music, I am immediately uplifted.

» Be honest with yourself if you are investing too much time into work and not enough time with people you love. Take the time to nurture your most important relationships—it is the people we love that ground us, provide us with purpose, and keep us inspired to be a better person.

» If your challenges are overwhelming, consider therapy with a professional to help you gain perspective and insights to move forward.

» Given the four challenges outlined at the beginning of this chapter and their impact on the future of work, what can you do to solve these challenges in your workplace?

You are reading this book and you made it to this chapter (congrats!). As you have read through this chapter, what has sparked you to focus on your "what's next?"

Do you need to focus on being more flexible as a leader and build your abilities to navigate the fast pace of change?

Are you challenged right now with finding and keeping good people?

Are you struggling with staying inspired because you are dealing with multiple generational teams and feel stuck?

As we look at navigating the future, the very first step is to decide what your next step is.

Take the time to complete this questionnaire—a detailed version is in the companion workbook (also available online) to help you determine what's next for you/your team/your company:

WHAT'S YOUR NEXT QUESTIONNAIRE:

1. What are the current challenges you are facing right now?
   a. Dealing with fast pace of change.
   b. Dealing with high turnover of people.
   c. Dealing with differing generational viewpoints.
   d. Dealing with competitive pressure.

2. When you think of the future, which of these statements is true for you?
   e. I am optimistic and excited.
   f. I am optimistic and anxious.
   g. I am optimistic and fatalistic.
   h. I am anxious and afraid.

3. If money were no object, what would you choose to do?
   i. Stay where I am—I love what I do.
   j. Leave my job and start my own business.
   k. Leave my job and start a non-profit.
   l. I would not work at all.

4. When you think of robots, AI, and automation, which of these statements/questions is true for you?

   m. Bring on the robots—I can have a personal assistant.

   n. What about me? Will I have a job?

   o. What do I need to learn to be ready?

   p. What impact will these technologies have on next generations?

5. When you think of where you are now and the change you know needs to happen in your company, which of the actions do you think you need to take first?

   q. We need to strategize with the leadership about next steps to be future ready.

   r. We need to provide all of our leaders with coaching and support to be future ready.

   s. We need to bring in an outside perspective to help us navigate the future.

   t. We need to rally the troops and reconnect them to vision, purpose, and direction.

There are no right answers to this questionnaire; the purpose is for you to take a pulse of where you and your company are and from there decide on the immediate next step.

In Part Three I will provide the NextMapping™ process and how you can use it to fully flesh out your "next."

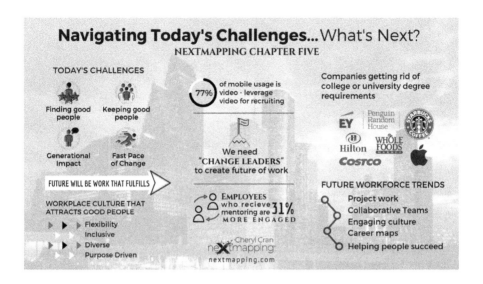

https://nextmapping.com/nextmapping-infographics-download/

PART THREE

CREATE THE FUTURE OF WORK

CHAPTER SIX

CREATE A CULTURE OF TRUST TO CREATE THE FUTURE OF WORK

"The most valuable business commodity is trust."

Richard Branson

In order to create the future of work, there needs to be a cultural foundation of trust.

There is science-backed research that proves that a trust culture has higher rates of engagement and other benefits.

Paul J. Zak, a Harvard researcher, found there is a direct relationship between trust, leadership, and organizational performance. Zak discovered that people at high trust companies have 74% less stress, 13% fewer sick days, 50% higher productivity, 106% more energy, and 40% less burnout.

Zak also found there is a direct correlation between the amount of "feel-good" hormone oxytocin a person's brain produces and the level of trust someone experiences.

With a decade of research, Zak found that oxytocin levels decrease significantly when we feel stress. His research also revealed a link between oxytocin levels and empathy, which is essential for a trust culture.

Empathy is a crucial future-of-work skill that is part of the human intelligence skills needed to increase connection and trust within teams.

Zak provides eight strategies or behaviors that induce trust within a culture.

A brief overview of the strategies includes:

1. A culture of recognizing excellence—neuroscience proves that public recognition has the biggest impact on trust when it happens right after an employee meets a goal.

2. Create "positive challenge stress" by setting reasonable and attainable goals, which boosts oxytocin, creating deeper focus and collaboration.

3. Empower a workplace of "choice" where employees have autonomy over work and have control over their work environment.

4. Invite employees to co-design their job—employees thrive when given the opportunity to have input on projects, to have a say about who they work with, and how they complete their work.

5. Constant communication—trust increases with thorough and frequent communication. Daily communication with direct reports increases trust exponentially.

6. Encourage intentional relationships—a LinkedIn study revealed that almost 50% of professionals believe that having work friends is critical to overall happiness.

7. Provide whole person growth opportunities—trust is increased when an employee feels that he or she is being given comprehensive personal and professional development beyond technical development.

8. Be open and vulnerable—trust increases when there is a commitment to truth and safety. <u>Brene Brown has an excellent TED Talk</u> on the power of vulnerability as a way of being and building trust.

The only way to create the future of work is with a foundation of trust, and to ensure that you as a leader or team member are invoking trust, as well as an organizational focus on increasing trust within the workplace.

Some questions to ask about your current company culture are:

1. Do we have a culture where it's safe for people to bring up a concern?

2. Do we have a culture where it's okay for people to fail?

3. Do we have a culture that encourages autonomy within a job?

4. Do we have a culture that encourages different ways of working? (i.e. remote/in office/etc.)

5. Do we have a culture where our leaders coach and grow people?

6. Do we have a culture where we reward performance in a public way?

7. Do we have a culture where we communicate often and openly?

8. Do we have a culture that takes care of people while we go through change?

If you answered mostly "No," then you already know you have a major challenge ahead. Your "next," quite simply, would be to meet with the leadership and HR teams and make a huge commitment to creating a higher trust culture.

If you answered yes to some of the questions with a few no's, you will want to use the questions that you answered "no" to as your baseline for NextMapping™ your future in regard to shoring up a trust culture.

Trust is critical in the workplace, especially in times of intense and fast change. With the increase of robotics, automation, and AI, many people are feeling worried about their work future and are fearful of losing money, autonomy, and security.

> *As leaders, we need to take control of the future by leading the changes needed to create the future. Regardless of title, everyone needs to take a lead in his or her personal future and also as an influencer in the company.*

INCREASING TECHNOLOGY AND ITS IMPACT ON TRUST

Employees surveyed are pretty optimistic about the future and about the role of technology. They believe that technology will keep evolving and provide new and different benefits within the workplace. Some of the "predictions" made by people we have surveyed include:

» Voice recognition will replace keyboards

» Tablets will replace laptops

» Computers will be used with hand gestures

» Keyboards and mouses will be obsolete

At face value these changes could create concern about the need for so many people in the workplace. However, those advancements in technology will not replace people in the workplace.

The positive impact of increasing technology innovation on trust in the workplace is that increased technology and more integrative ways of working allow people to work by their own design.

Business leaders, IT leaders, and HR leaders all have an opportunity to focus on better understanding their employees' diverse needs and provide the right technology, resources, and environments to do their best work.

The six areas to ensure that employees are set up to succeed, feel part of a trust culture, and feel supported include:

Technology – provide the right technology for the job, which may mean multiple devices and multiple applications.

Easy Access – provide employees with easy access to data and applications from any device, anywhere, and at any time.

Secure Access – provide secure data for BYOD (bring your own device) and ensure that all access is secured and identity protected.

Diverse Locations – as technology continues to innovate the way work gets done, people have stronger desires to choose when and where they meet their professional obligations. Provide the tools and collaboration that enable them to be effective in any environment.

Diverse Workspace – the days of the walled-in offices are going away—provide employees with workspace options within the workplace. This includes having private rooms for phone calls, open collaboration spaces, game spaces, and meeting spaces.

Remote and In-Office Collaboration – provide your remote and in-office teams with ways to collaborate effectively. Leverage tools, such as Slack, Workplace by Facebook, Yammer, and other tools make it easy for both internal and external employees to connect and collaborate.

STYLE OF LEADERSHIP THAT INVOKES TRUST

With the increase of media on workplaces, such as in the film industry and the #metoo movement, there is a stronger awareness among leaders of the need to ensure that leaders are operating with full integrity.

Organizational cultures that focus on leadership development, including diversity and inclusion training as well as workplace harassment training, tend to have a higher trust culture.

Leaders need to have a more meaningful and conscious approach to employee engagement and create a "safe" culture of "see something and say something" without punishment or rebuke.

In an open, shared leadership culture, it is encouraged for all team members to speak up in a respectful way if he or she sees or hears something that is uncomfortable or insensitive to anyone in the company.

If challenging situations or interactions are brought to light with respect and a willingness to make the culture even better, it is good for the business and employees overall.

The leadership attributes that invoke trust include:

» Integrity – the leader walks his or her talk—promises made are kept.

» Inclusion – respecting gender, generation, ethnicity, culture, and uniqueness.

» Flexible – provides options for how to work and when to work.

» Clarity – provides clear outlines for expectations.

» Truth – tells the truth about challenges and company status.

» Growth – helps team members grow and learn beyond basic job.

» Inspiration – inspires through stories and recognition.

» Candid Communication – direct yet caring.

» Developmental Feedback – gives specific feedback with ideas for success.

» Accountable – willing to be held accountable for words and actions.

Take a few moments to review the above list—if you were to rate yourself as a leader (whether your title is leader or not) on a scale of one to ten, with ten being the highest, what would you give yourself?

If you rated yourself six or lower on any of the items on the above list, those items become part of your personal goal planning over the next ninety days.

For example, if you gave yourself a five for candid communication, you can set personal goals to hone that skill over the next three months.

Research resources for each of the items, and then focus on improving in that area. Once ninety days is up, go to the next item that you rated six or lower, and this is your next personal goal.

At the back of the book in the Resource section, you will see more resources, websites, and recommendations to support you.

A culture of trust increases the ability of teams to increase their bandwidth to be more creative, to innovate more quickly, and to leverage disagreements into breakthrough ideas.

Imagine your company consisted primarily of people who had an abundant mindset, who had high levels of self-worth, who had optimistic expectations of the future, and who had a strong passion to work collaboratively.

If your company already has abundant-minded people who are optimistic about creating the future, then you are in the top ten percent of companies globally.

If your company does not have an abundant-minded trust culture, make plans to take action toward creating the foundational culture needed to create the future of work.

HIGH TRUST CULTURE LEADS TO INNOVATION

If your work culture has high trust factor and your leaders have the attributes of a trusted leader, it is likely that your company is doing very well and you have highly satisfied customers and highly engaged employees.

We can't talk about creating the future of work without talking about creating a trust culture because the two go hand in hand.

The interpersonal dynamics of a high trust culture goes way beyond the basics of communication—people strive to be their best and therefore build new skills and capabilities. Organizations that have a culture where leaders and teams operate with greater trust have greater freedom for leaders and teams to create and innovate.

A company that has an embedded trust culture creates an environment for leaders and teams to innovate with free reign and potentially transform the future of the business.

For example, Kyle Nels, founder and former executive director of Lowe's Innovation Labs, was given free reign by Lowe's and complete autonomy (trust) to develop the Innovation Lab the way he wanted.

The result is that under Kyle's leadership Lowe's had many innovations, including the in-store robot I mentioned earlier in this book. Fast Company named Lowe's Innovation Lab as a top innovator in 2018.

Nels attributes the success of the Lowe's Innovation Lab to the team's ability to think in very unique and different ways that he calls "divergent thinking." At first, senior leadership did not like the idea of a "robot"— they felt it was too impersonal. Senior leadership trusted the innovation team and voiced a concern about losing the personal touch with customers. Nels was able to invoke trust in his innovation team's idea by using the power of a compelling story, which incorporated animation and the simulation of a robot in store to help senior leadership see the potential of the innovation and impact on customer experience.

Nels's team had the autonomy to use divergent thinking to communicate the entire concept using animation, real customer scenarios, and video of the test robot interacting with clients. Where most retailers were focusing on self-checkouts, Nels's team went a few steps further to create a customer service robot.

In a high trust culture, there is an energy of "openness" to all types of things that are different. In fact, *it is the differences that lead to the innovations.* In many current organizations, there is still a prevalent culture of protecting legacy systems or projects and a reluctance to invest and focus on wacky, out-of-the-box ideas.

> *One of our goals at NextMapping™ is to help leaders and teams tackle the barriers to innovation and breakthrough growth, which include lack of trust culture and complete shift in thinking about current business and the future of work.*

In addition to divergent thinking, Kyle Nels and his team encouraged healthy confrontation. With innovation, sometimes the most radical idea can come from a disagreement. The skill that this requires is "confrontational tolerance," the ability to handle confrontation without taking it personally.

Confrontational tolerance requires individuals to have healthy self-esteem and the ability to see disagreement as an innovation marker, not something that needs to be defended.

When you have teams with healthy confrontational tolerance, you have individuals who are able to remain highly effective in an environment of people strongly expressing opposing views.

For example, you could be part of a project team, and you as a team member have come up with a brilliant idea to improve on a customer service deliverable. You are excited about the idea, but you are worried about "Nelly" on the team, who you know for sure is going to poke holes in your idea. With strong confrontational tolerance as a skill, you do not worry about pushback or anyone poking holes because you have built a health awareness that all pushback is good in that it will only make the idea or the process better in the end.

In fact, as you build your confrontational muscle, you look forward to the contribution of ideas that are opposed to your own, and you welcome engaging in spirited and productive debates with others over your own and their ideas.

The attributes of someone with high confrontational tolerance are:

» Open-minded and willingness to hear opposing ideas.

» Willing to respectfully debate an idea.

» Flexible to adapting a personal idea with input.

» Able to communicate effectively during a disagreement.

» Able to move on and have healthy relationships with others that oppose or disagree.

» Expects others to see what he or she can't see and to provide objective input.

» Appreciates divergent thinking and sees it as it always leading to the best end product or service enhancement.

Teams that consist of people who have developed his or her confrontational tolerance are able to drive change and innovation at a faster and more effective pace.

When someone disagrees with an idea, it's an opportunity to investigate the opposing perspective and find out if there is validity to the point being made.

At this stage, for me personally, disagreement is a "sign" for me to pay very close attention—not for ways to protect what I have come up with. Rather listen for something I may be missing or something that could make the project or service even better.

This is listening with an "innovation ear," rather than with a "protectionist bias ear."

Listening with an "innovation ear" means:

» Remaining open-minded and curious when faced with disagreement or criticism.

» Thinking of ways to "poke" holes at the idea with intent of making end product or service even better.

» Looking for patterns and symbols from disagreement that could lead to greater scope of opportunity.

» Respecting multiple perspectives and humbly acknowledging that we are but a single perspective.

» Noticing my need to protect the idea as I have presented it and allow myself to flex to others' input on the idea

You will know you are listening with a protectionist bias ear when you won't listen; you push back and forge ahead without considering input or feedback.

LEAD CHANGE EFFORTLESSLY WITH A HIGH TRUST CULTURE

The only way to create the future of work is through change. Change of attitude, change of approach, change to structures, and change toward a new way of working and interacting with people.

One of my most popular keynotes has been one based on my book, *The Art of Change Leadership – Driving Transformation in a Fast-Paced World*. The keynote is titled, "Leading Change in a Fast-Paced and Technological Workplace," and in it I present research and strategies on how to create a "culture" that consists of change leaders.

There are a few myths about change that include:

1. Change can only happen from the top down.

2. Change needs to be project managed.

3. Change needs everyone to "buy in."

These myths actually hinder the progress toward sustainable change.

The counter truths to these myths are:

1. Change can start from any person or department within the organization.

2. Change requires a "platform" of inclusion and collaboration to be successful.

3. Change needs people to be engaged and connected to the reasons for change.

The reason that 70% of change initiatives fail is because of belief about the myths about change.

The reason change is difficult is because humans inherently do not *trust* change.

Human beings have brains that are wired to react with sudden change; the fight-or-flight response is part of our survival mechanism. Think of the last time you went through a sudden change and you will remember that your immediate instinct is to either push back or run away.

A trust culture creates an environment where it is safe to change, it is okay to build toward the future, and even though the future is somewhat unknown, there are ways in which to build some control and positive outcomes.

In fact, where there is safety and trust, change DOES happen almost as an outcome of people wanting to innovate and create for the future. Often when changes are dictated from the top down, they are met with cynicism and fear because it appears as an agenda, rather than a change that will benefit people, namely clients and employees.

Making sustainable and innovative change requires a movement, not a mandate.

LEAD CHANGE BY CREATING A MOVEMENT

A movement is created when a group of people forms around a cause or a dissatisfaction to create change. With a movement there is emotion, connection, and a desire to create something better than what was in place before.

A movement within a company can happen from a small group of people within a department or can happen from a project team. When leaders mandate a change, it creates an automatic psychological response of "push back."

Think about this from a personal level—if someone tells you that you HAVE to change something, your immediate reaction is likely going to be, "No, I don't!" In a movement, there is a compelling vision and goal that invites you to participate and provides you with options and levels of participation.

A trust culture allows movements to arise because the "energy" of the company is of allowing, mentoring, learning, and growing from mistakes or failures.

A movement provides an emotional connection toward creating something positive in the future, and with the right focus, you can shift the outcome of a change project by framing it as a movement, rather than a "forced change."

Therefore, if you were trying to get your entire company to adopt a new cloud-based solution, for example, you would want to frame it as a movement.

The components of creating a movement are:

» Gather input from everyone on the desired future of having across-the-board adoption of the new cloud-based solution.

» Aggregate the input and share the common desired future with everyone.

» Create a contest for employees to "name" the movement and announce the winner.

» Publicize the winner and the name of the movement, i.e., ice bucket challenge for ALS.

» Create a video that explains the purpose of the movement (change), make it a story, and use video of employees sharing their "why" they are with the movement.

» Create an animated version of the purpose of the movement and share with teams through intranet and in meetings.

» Identify key influencers and inspire them to engage teams with the movement.

» Start with a beta team of cheerleaders/early adopters and have them gain momentum by sharing stories and celebrations of progress of cloud adoption impact.

» Rotate movement leaders who communicate and update on progress.

» Create dialogues and opportunities for venting and talking about challenges or hiccups of the movement as it progresses.

» Movements take time to gain momentum—be willing to remain committed to keeping the movement top of mind and on pace with original desired vision.

» Once the movement is complete, have a celebration of the end of Project X, and then look to move focus to the next movement.

The compelling reason to leverage movements for big change is that movements contribute to building a trust culture. There is less fear and pushback and more involvement and eagerness to embrace a change mindset and look at movements as moving projects.

As you make progress toward either creating a trust-based culture or increasing the trust factor within your business, you will find that there are direct payoffs. What you will begin to notice with an increasing trust culture is:

» More people speaking openly and honestly about fears and challenges.

» More people willing to risk and ask important questions.

» More people respectfully challenging each other to ensure best outcomes for client, team, and company.

» More people engaged with the company overall.

» More people willing to share ideas and to innovate.

» More people working together collaboratively.

» Increased business and client satisfaction as a result of happier employees.

Now that we have looked at trust culture as foundation of creating the future, the next chapter will focus on the human/robot/AI/automation dynamic and how to create your future with the best integration of all of these dynamics.

https://nextmapping.com/nextmapping-infographics-download/

CHAPTER SEVEN

A VERY HUMAN FUTURE WITH ROBOTS, AI, AND AUTOMATION

"I believe the future of work will finally set free the greatest asset we have: human intelligence. This will require systems that are smart enough to enable human critical thinking at scale."

Steven ZoBell – CTO Workforce

In my whitepaper, which you can download on "If the Future of Work Is about Robots – What Does It Mean for Humans?" I provide research on the impact of robots, AI, and automation on the future of work, as well as what it means for jobs of the future and the future of work.

There is a lot of research that confirms that many repeatable task jobs are either being replaced now or will be in the short-term future. This can create fear in many people because the obvious concern is what about my job or how will I pay my bills?

There is also a lot of counter research that states that the rise of automation, AI, and robots will create new and different opportunities for humans.

Let's take a look at both sides of the equation:

Robots, automation, and AI WILL take over jobs and tasks.

A <u>study conducted by McKinsey</u> Global found that by 2030, 800 million jobs could be lost to automation. In the US, 39 to 73 million jobs stand to be automated, which equates to about a third of the workforce.

The report cites that about 5% of ALL current jobs are to be automated, while today, 60% of current jobs there will be about one third that stand to be automated in the future. A pull-out quote from the McKinsey report states that:

"Technology destroys jobs, but not work."

The researchers of the report point to the after-effects of the personal computer when it was launched in 1980. The personal computer led to the creation of 18.5 million new jobs, even when accounting for jobs that were lost.

However, we cannot apply the same logic to industrial robots with reports that indicate jobs will be lost. A study by the National Bureau of Economic Research looked at the historical effects of robots on employment in the US.

The study looked at the historical effect of robots on the US labor market between 1990 and 2007 and studied the effect of robots on employment rates in a variety of areas. The study revealed that for each new robot added to the workforce, there were three to five jobs lost by humans. Put simply—one robot can do the work of up to five people. From a productivity and profitability standpoint you can see the compelling case for industries to embrace robotics as a solution to labor shortage.

The industries hardest hit with the impact of industrial robots are "blue collar," including manufacturing and construction. Jobs that are experiencing the robot influx effect are blue collar workers, routine manual occupations, assembly line workers, machinists, and transport workers.

The study goes on to clarify that in the US, the rise of industrial robots has been limited. The prediction is that over the next two decades, as more industries implement the use of industrial robots, we will see a continued impact and effect on jobs.

Current research on the impact of robots, automation, and AI includes data from the McKinsey study of 2017, which states it may not be a total of 800 million jobs replaced, but more of a middle ground of 400 million.

The McKinsey study is one of the most in-depth in recent years and included changes in over 800 occupations in forty-six countries. Nations included in the study: Mexico, US, China, Germany, Japan, and India.

The McKinsey report points out that the countries hardest hit by job loss due to robotics are Germany and the US. Both of these countries have employers that pay higher wages and are incentivized toward automation. The jobs that will be automated will be jobs held by middle- and low-skilled occupations. The prediction is a double-tiered labor market, where higher income workers will have the resources to adapt more readily.

The report gives historical review of the US's transition away from agriculture and decrease in farming jobs has led to an increase in spending on secondary education. Also, there were new laws that instituted compulsory school attendance. In 1910, eighteen percent of teenagers went to high school, and by 1940, seventy-three percent of teenagers were in high school.

The shift in focus away from working the farm as a teenager and toward increased education helped create a major boom in manufacturing and a thriving middle class. Today we require a push to help workers reskill and upskill in order to build agility and ability to create new jobs and opportunities in the future of work.

Currently, data states that in six out of ten jobs, 30% of activities are automatable.

Automation and AI will lift productivity and economic growth, but millions of people worldwide will likely need to switch occupations or upgrade skills.

Let's now look at the counterview that:

ROBOTS, AUTOMATION, AND **AI WILL CREATE** NEW JOBS.

The same McKinsey report cited above states that new jobs WILL be created. Existing jobs will be redefined, and workers will have the opportunity to completely switch careers. The biggest challenge for workers is managing the transition from current reality to future reality. What's needed is a massive movement for organizations to provide change in leadership support, training, and learning opportunities.

Workers need to seek upskilling or reskilling through employers as well as be willing to invest in their own education, learning, and growth in order to be future ready. The good news is that if a robot or automation does take your job or you think that your current job will be replaced in the future, you can have the opportunity to prepare and create a new future.

Employers will be seeking workers who can work alongside robots, who are able to leverage AI and automation. The robotics movement actually helps solve a longstanding problem for many industries right now, which is the ability to find good people to do current jobs. In industries such as manufacturing, there is a mass exodus of baby boomer workers at retirement age. Although research shows that baby boomers will work beyond traditional retirement age of sixty-five, many are continuing to work on a contract basis but in a less strenuous type job.

For example, the number of retirees that drive for Uber and Lyft is significantly high, as many retirees seek to augment retirement income and stay social. Research by Market Watch states that 51% of Uber and Lyft drivers are over fifty-one years of age. More Uber drivers are over fifty than under thirty, and Uber has joined with AARP to offer sign-up bonuses for older drivers.

In the US, the McKinsey report predicts that employment in industries such as healthcare will continue to increase as the rise of the aging population increases.

Care providers, such as doctors, nurses, pharmacists, therapists, social workers, and other healthcare professionals, are set to see major growth in opportunities with an 83% growth in Mexico, 242% growth in India, 122% growth in China, and 30% growth in the US.

Another industry poised to be booming is the wellness industry as people seek health solutions outside of traditional healthcare.

High-paying creative jobs will be at a premium.

Jobs for creatives are set to grow by 85% in China, 58% in India, and 28% in Mexico. The opportunities to create a different future are only limited by the willingness to make minor or major changes. In addition to reskilling or upskilling, there are opportunities to look at working in other countries or working FOR a company in another country virtually or remotely from your home office.

One of the fast-growing jobs sectors is in the technology sector—technology professions in the US are set to grow by 34% and in India 129%.

Teaching jobs will increase by 9% in the US, but by a whopping 208% in India and 119% in China.

Management and leadership opportunities are growing too—75% growth in India, 40% in China, 24% in Mexico, 21% in Germany, and 15% in the US. So right now, as you read this, if you are a leader, you have great future job security IF you continue to upskill and reskill. If you are not a leader, you have the current opportunity to learn and grow and find out all you can about being a future-ready leader.

The building profession, which includes engineers, architects, and construction workers, is set to grow by 35% in the US, 48% in Mexico, and a whopping 117% in India. Other professionals that include business and financial specialists, legal industry, scientists, and academics will experience modest growth at 11% in the US and 26% in China.

Interestingly enough, jobs that may be declining in certain markets are increasing in other markets. For example, in the US there is predicted a decline in administrative assistant jobs, procurement, and payroll. However, countries that will be looking to fill these jobs include Mexico, India, and China.

Given there is research that says some jobs will be lost, it is important to clarify that with some tasks automated, employment in those jobs may not decline, but rather workers may be doing completely different and newer tasks.

Jobs such as managing people, applying expertise, and social interactions will be difficult to automate as machines are unable to match human performance . . . for now!

AMAZON HYBRID HUMAN/ROBOT WORKPLACE

More than twenty-five of Amazon's 175 fulfillment centers use robotics, or about 100,000 robots.

In an Amazon warehouse, humans and robots work alongside each other to fulfill orders. Amazon's warehouses have been partially automated for some time with a growing number of Kiva robots being used to carry products to human workers who select items to be shipped to customers.

Interestingly, facilities with robots tend to employ more humans because they are more efficient at processing orders. With automation impacting almost all industries, as mentioned earlier, manufacturing is seeing major changes.

Thirteen percent of manufacturing firms have already adopted collaborative robots (co-bots). According to ABI, research robots in warehouses are expected to jump by fifteen times over the next three years. Many experts predict that robots will continue to be allies for humans and free humans up to do higher-level tasks, rather than be completely replaced.

Amazon's warehouse in Monee has more than 2,000 full-time employees working along with Kiva robots, delivering items to workers. Amazon states that the expansion of robots has led to more jobs and more investments. The robot influence in warehouses is felt in the way that they have taken over the "heavy lifting" elements of the job. The robots do all the work that humans either dislike doing or are at risk of being injured. Tasks like moving boxes, picking products from shelves, and packing boxes with the help of humans.

In addition to the human/robot hybrid, there is a shift toward workers wanting to work in environments that are technologically enabled. The future is very human in that workers are seeking a new kind of workspace.

Workers Seeking SMART Workplaces

A study conducted by HP on the digital workforce has found that employees WANT digital transformation and automation.

Sixty-four percent of employees surveyed thought that their organization risks falling behind if new technology is not integrated. Seventy-one percent surveyed feel strongly that the workplace should be automated.

Increasingly workers are looking for digitally integrated workplaces and so, just like the shift toward smart homes, employees are looking to work in smart workplaces. Seventy-two percent of workers surveyed stated that the workplace should be completely interactive and have the ability to automatically update and adjust to workers' requests.

Like a smart home, people want to work in a digitally powered environment that can adjust office climate, book meetings using voice commands, deliver packages by indoor drones, and more.

WORKERS SEEKING SOUL-SOOTHING WORKSPACES

In a technology-enabled workspace, workers are seeking to have the technology tools at their fingertips, AND they are seeking to be able to work in a soul-soothing environment.

In a 2018 survey by Clutch, the top five items workers are seeking from their workspace are:

1. 61% of workers want to work in an aesthetically pleasing work-space.
2. 39% want the option of a dedicated office or work space.
3. 53% value having a variety of locations to work in.
4. 25% want flexible work space options and do NOT have flex work options.
5. 47% value a community workspace (the chance to interact with others).

Characteristics of an aesthetically pleasing workspace include open, airy, and modern, greenery, and natural lighting.

The continued pace of rapid change toward robotics, automation, and technological innovation means more opportunities for humans to do what they do best, and this is to be HUMAN.

Klaus Schwab of the World Economic forum says work should not be a race between humans and machines but a part of life that helps people realize their full potential.

Humans More Valuable Than Technology

The human/robot/AI/Automated hybrid is going to elevate business and informed decisions. Already data is expanding daily at an exponential rate. Organizations are harvesting their most valuable data, which are the behaviors of their clients and employees. As organizations gather more data about their clients and employees, they are able to innovate more rapidly and apply data insights to strategic plans.

However, humans are still the end decision makers, while CEOs and leaders will use real-time data about sales, cash flow, and threats from competitors to gain insights. It will be easier for senior leadership teams to get concrete business intelligence from technology solutions. AI-infused programs use current and past data to provide a heads up and recommend solutions to improve business.

There isn't an app or robot that is going to make the final decision on strategy, expansion, or whether to initiate a merger. AI will provide input, and ultimately senior leadership, along with informed input from crowdsourced clients and employees, will set the course to create the future.

As robots evolve and gather more data about strategies that work and don't work, they could make decisions come 2030, and a human workforce would likely take instruction from them. The biggest challenge for the future job of a CEO is still going to be getting the most out of a human/robot hybrid workforce.

CEOs and senior leadership will have to be more transparent and create more trust than ever before to lead the fast-changing future of work.

Experts say that human talent becomes more valuable as technology innovation grows. It will be humans who will leverage technology to drive organizations to succeed.

A study commissioned by Korn Ferry found that human talent is 2.33 times more valuable than physical capital, including inventory, real estate, and technology. The study included eight countries, and in each country the story is the same. The report states that technology-centric places like Silicon Valley will have human capital $182 trillion more valuable than physical capital.

The study goes on to point out two reasons people outperform the most sophisticated technology—potential and appreciation. A human's potential is not fixed like a physical asset (including robots); human potential grows and expands. As people upskill, reskill, and enhance performance, they bring more value to the business over time. Machines, including robots, depreciate over time.

The risk to business today is to operate and strategize from a "technological blind spot," which is to value technology over people.

Leaders are facing increased pressure to generate performance and can fall into the trap of focusing on technology as the holy grail of solutions. This is a mistake—the future that is created needs to be built with a human/people perspective.

Technology alone is not the solution that organizations seek. The tools of the digital age are amazing, but overall productivity has not yet increased. Investing in human capital generates greater economic output.

Airbnb is a great example of enabling people with technology, rather than replacing them. In fact, Airbnb democratized access for people, and the main vision when Airbnb was created was to "help people visit the world through the eyes of a local." Started as a home-sharing platform, they have now added tour guides and experiences provided by locals in the city that a guest is visiting. When technology increases connection and opportunity for people, it is serving the best possible future.

Airbnb has about 3,000 people on payroll, but thousands of talented humans are hosts to over two million rooms worldwide, and the new ancillary services reaches out to thousands more.

A great example of technology that was created to solve a human problem. Ultimately, as technology solutions increase, we as humans will be seeking more HUMAN solutions and experiences as a result.

FUTURE NEEDS LEADERS WHO ARE MORE HUMAN

Trends that will continue to impact the future include increasing diversity among teams. Leaders will be navigating an increase in diverse teams, multi-generational teams, and teams with a wide array of values and personalities.

Leaders will need to help their human workforce to lead change and increase flexibility and resiliency. In fact, leaders who help to create a workplace where people can rest and restore and rejuvenate will be on the leading edge of a future workplace.

Human skills, such as emotional intelligence, personality intelligence, and other intelligences, as outlined previously in this book, will be the premium skills that leaders will need to upgrade. Leaders who develop their persuasion and influencing skills will be in higher demand in the future. The ability to "share power" is going to be a game changer for leaders and teams in the future of work.

A key strategic focus needs to be investing in reskilling and upskilling workers rather than simply looking to hire more workers.

According to a survey of Chief Human Resources Officers (CHROs), 65% said their CEOs are investing in reskilling of their employees.

In 2030, the CEO will still be human, according to current research. The role of the CEO will change dramatically based on rapidity of change and the human/robot hybrid factor.

Humans have the ability to create context, whereas robots create information and data. It's one thing to have abundance of information and another to be able to discern and direct what to DO with the information that has been created.

The fear that technology is going to replace humans needs perspective and reskilling. When you think of innovations of the past, it has progressively always increased work for humans. Think of the innovations of train travel, air travel, and the personal computer as examples. Each of these innovations created new work and new types of work.

To add further thinking about how technology is impacting the future of types of work for humans in the future, here are ten jobs that didn't exist ten years ago:

1. Social media manager
2. Uber driver
3. Cloud computing specialist
4. Sustainability manager
5. Millennial generation expert

6. App developer

7. Driverless car engineer

8. Big data analyst

9. YouTube content creators

10. Drone operators

HUMAN EMOTIONS PROVIDE KEY DATA FOR THE FUTURE

Data on its own is simply information, but what if we could contextualize information from our clients and employees by understanding emotional responses?

Behavioral scientists are making this a reality for businesses. Recently I interviewed Dr. Thomas Ramsey of <u>Neurons Inc</u> for my NextMapping™ podcast, and his insights into the future of gathering contextual information was fascinating.

How the Neurons Inc technology works is a device with electrodes is placed on the head and measures emotional responses.

Kyle Nels, formerly of Lowe's, worked with Neurons Inc to help test reactions to innovations that were being created in the Lowe's Innovation lab. What they found is that if an idea was provided to a group of clients, for example, they might say what they think but are filtering their responses. What the device does is provide real-time data on whether a person is excited or not interested, and so it gives more accurate visceral responses.

The ramifications of this technology are far reaching when you consider that you could have everyone in your next team meeting wearing this head device and very quickly would be able to see if people were on board or not. Basically, the head device technology bypasses the conscious and measures subconscious reactions or what someone is "really" thinking. Imagine having this device in your meetings—can you see that there would be more "truth" in the discussions?

Humans are emotional; robots cannot replicate or duplicate human emotions. The fear mongers would say the frightening part of robotics is what if they can eventually understand human emotional complexity?

Dr. Nigel Shadbolt, professor of computer science at Oxford University, says that robots will never rise up but rather become part of daily living.

He goes on to say that children today will be growing up with robot friends and the elderly will have robot caregivers. Fears that machines will become sentient and harmful are not based on fact. Hollywood would have us believe that AI is a threat to humanity and that we don't want to get close to robots.

We should not fear AI; we should fear the humans programming them! Or as Dr. Shadbolt says, fear "natural stupidity."

The robots and AI that are being created are programmed for super narrow tasks and one form of super intelligence that is data based. Right now AI does not know how to transfer from one task to another. In other words, it can only work one program at a time that it has been programmed to do.

Because we as humans are emotional beings, we project onto robots and AI and begin to empathize with them. Therefore, humans will be developing companionship rather than rivalry with robots in the future. I mentioned earlier the carebots caring for patients—research was done to show that those being lifted or supported formed a "bond" with the robot.

Affinity with our support tools creates emotional connections—think about how you felt the last time you misplaced your smartphone. Panic stricken? Afraid? Lost?

Smartphones are one of the greatest technological advances of the modern age; they are the supercomputers in our pockets, but the smartphone does not understand how amazing it is. It just exists as a supercomputer at our disposal that will do whatever we ask it to do.

HUMANS CREATING THE FUTURE OF WORK

Now that we can breathe easy knowing that we can't blame the robots for our future, we can focus on what WE are going to do to create the future.

Recent research done by Catalant has found that 63% of CEOs surveyed have a future of work program. Fifty-two percent stated that the CHRO and the CEO are key drivers focused on creating the future of work.

Organizations ARE focusing on the reskilling and upskilling of their workers with 53% investing in developing an agile workforce, versus investing 19% in AI and automation.

As organizations invest in solutions for humans, including clients and employees, 84% of executives surveyed admit that they have not yet tapped into the talent, new ideas, and capabilities of people. More organizations are taking heed of the trend toward entrepreneurial workers and the rise of co-working spaces and seeking to create more workspace options to keep talent engaged.

Forty-three percent of HR leaders report that they are behind or way behind the changes needed to be future of work ready in their workplace.

The struggle for talent continues in that one in two talent leaders surveyed reported that openings for critical roles remained unfilled for at least ninety days. This has resulted in lost productivity because of the "human talent gap."

Adding to the challenge of finding good people, 44% of HR leaders say they do not have enough training to take advantage of the future of work, and 37% say that they can't find the right technology to capitalize on the future of work.

From a human perspective, the number of digital platforms is booming, but 77% of leaders surveyed admit they can't name two of them! So, the technology is there, but the human capacity to leverage is still lacking.

To create the very human future of work, here are eight key insights on what must be done to create the next level of success and the future of work:

1. Change continues to be the barrier to humans doing a better and faster job of innovating—leaders need to provide change leadership learning for leaders and teams in order to increase ability to navigate ongoing and persistent change.

2. Focus needs to be on aligning the leadership and teams' mindsets—regular communication on the "why" and the "how" needs to be happening.

3. Companies need to be focused on the "future of work" as an initiative and just like an innovation lab needs to develop a "create the future of work" lab within the organization.

4. Thirty-four percent of leaders mention that finding the right cultural fit is the roadblock to leveraging "on demand" talent—leaders need to be able to articulate and inspire culture in order to identify the right cultural fit early on.

5. Before mainstreaming new technology tools, make sure you manage the integration like a "change management" project—the biggest barrier to technology uptake is underestimating the amount of

"human" influencing that needs to be done to increase uptake and mass buy in.

6. It's a very human future—what are you doing in your company to show that you value people over technology?

7. To create the future of work, organizations will have to make tough and bold moves to recreate the workplace, the culture, and changes required by humans to make the future a reality.

8. The companies that will successfully create the future will be those that view people/strategy as an integrated focus.

I personally get very inspired when I think of the future from the perspective of "human first." As long as leaders globally focus on strategy, organizational structures, and client services through the lens of "How does this help or serve people?" then we will leverage technology and digital transformation for the overall improvement of the world.

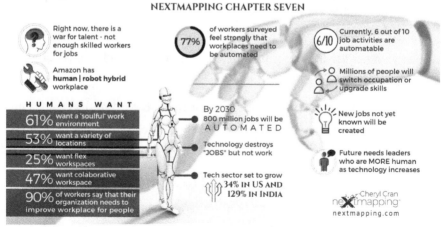

https://nextmapping.com/nextmapping-infographics-download/

CHAPTER EIGHT

NEXTMAPPING™ TO CREATE YOUR FUTURE OF WORK

"If you hesitate to map out your future, to make a big plan or to set a goal, you've just mapped out your future."

Seth Godin

Anticipating and navigating the future of work requires a plan, and that plan needs to be executed toward an end goal. Strategic plans and personal plans created today must have a focus on the future and the trends and shifts impacting the future.

This is not the time for "head in the sand" or hopeful thinking that your business or industry will be okay to keep going forward based on past success.

Research conducted by Innosight states that the average lifespan of a company has never been shorter. In 1965 the average lifespan of a Fortune 500 was thirty-three years, by 1990 it was twenty years, and by 2026, it is predicted it will shrink to 14%. This means that 40-50% of Fortune 500s will be replaced over the next ten years.

Traditionally, organizational transformation has happened from senior leadership and top down. Research from Gartner states that 42% of CEOs had started digital transformations in 2017. In our research and work with clients, we have found that organizational transformation happens with complete collaboration of all stakeholders within the company. Having senior leadership on board to transform the company is required. The key is to involve all people in the transformation in order for the company to truly transform.

I have worked with Gartner a number of times, and many of their conferences in the past have focused primarily on the IT and digitization of the workplace. For the past six years, they have been providing programs on leadership and the people dynamics as they recognize the inherent challenge in digital transformation is getting people to change and to get behind the changes. Organizations are realizing that in order to drive IT transformation they MUST be looking at digital transformation through the lens of involving people before the IT changes and leading the digitization process like a "change management" project.

Often the stumbling block to transforming the business is that the people who are asked to "work" toward transformation or change are the very ones that are affected by the change.

Many leaders are so focused on driving change forward that the much-needed step of gathering input and getting people on board with the "why" of the change is THE major stumbling block to transformation today.

An article in 1990 in Harvard Business Review stated that change and transformation that is grassroots has a stronger chance of success, and the same holds true for today and into the future. Grassroots change comes from demand from inside the organization and often from people who are closer to the problems. The "shared leadership" workplace that I have shared throughout this book creates a culture where change can happen from anyone and anywhere within the organization due to freedom to challenge, question, and put forward innovation ideas.

Organizational cultures that support a "grassroots change" environment supported by senior leadership are poised to be far more agile and competitive than those companies still modelling a "top-down" approach to transformation.

NextMapping™ to Create the Future

The best way to create the future is to have a plan that clearly maps out the steps and actions required for a compelling vision.

At NextMapping™, we have created our proprietary process that can be applied to ANY change or desired future.

The road signs for the map are:

Discover – In the discover phase of NextMapping™, we start with where you are now. This is where you and your teams invest in NextMapping™ research and identifying and articulating where you are now—your "current state."

We review your current strategic plan and the status of where you are now with your plan. If an organization does not have a current plan, then we use the NextMapping™ process to create a substantial and actionable NextMapping™ process plan.

The tools we use in the discover phase are varied and dependent on the specific dynamics of your situation. One of the tools we use in the discover phase is the WOW analysis, and WOW stands for:

What's Working?

What Are the Opportunities?

What's Next?

With the WOW analysis, we focus on leveraging current success. We don't spend an inordinate amount of time on "threats or weaknesses." We found that the obvious "gaps" show up when we focus on the "opportunities" section.

When we start with "what's working," it becomes very evident "what's not working," however by staying focused on the current successful strategies, our clients stay engaged with the process and remind themselves that they are already doing many things very well.

Many consultants belabor the weaknesses and threats, and while we do need to "poke holes" to ensure we have a well-thought-out approach, too much focus on threats can slow down the innovation and forward movement of creating the future. I facilitated SWOT (Strengths, Weaknesses, Opportunities, and Threats) analysis years ago, and the focus on threats and weaknesses can take the whole discussion and dialogue down the rabbit hole of everything that is wrong with the business. I have found this to waste a lot of precious time. Our WOW model has been successfully used many times with clients, as it keeps the focus on the now and the future in a positive and productive way.

Typically, in the past, organizations had their senior leaders do a SWOT analysis.

From there the senior leadership developed strategic plans and goals and then communicated them to their managers, who then communicated the goals to their teams.

This top-down approach to strategy or change typically results in lack of engagement and lack of buy in by both managers and employees.

Also, many organizations are still siloed when it comes to customer and employee survey data. They may be doing these surveys, however the results are not being fed into the strategic plan or communicated across the organization. The result is fragmented departments gathering data but not making efficient and successful use of the data that has been generated.

With the WOW process, we include the entire organization and clients in order to gather the most input and perspectives. We create a customized survey that is sent out to either employees only or sent to both employees and clients.

Included in the survey we gather work process facts (who, what, when, where) from the people who do the work to help identify gaps in structure or communication.

This survey is sent and data collated in advance of a strategic planning meeting that consists of leaders from each department along with senior leadership.

In the survey, in addition to the custom questions, we ask them to provide his or her perspective on WOW—what's working, what are the opportunities, and what's missing. The data we have gathered in this process is beyond eye opening. By gathering perspectives from throughout the company as well as clients, there are themes and obvious opportunities that arise.

Included in the discover part of the NextMapping™ process, we provide extensive research on your industry, your competitors, trends in "sister" industries, and creative potential with industries completely unlike yours.

Once we have gathered extensive data in the discover phase, THEN we have the foundation to continue forward with the NextMapping™ process. The next road sign is "ideate."

Ideate – With the ideate part of the roadmap, we now take the data that has been gathered and identify the patterns in the data. We also use the PREDICT model outlined in this book to generate ideas and "predictions."

A common challenge for an organization is that leaders and teams can be operating from a singular or limited perspective.

In the ideate phase, we are looking for common areas, such as frequent problems across departments, communication breakdowns, structural roadblocks, change responses with leaders and teams, and other patterns.

Often as humans we operate from one or two perspectives. For example, a leader may have a focus on self as a leader and another focus on his or her leader.

A senior executive may be focused solely on bottom line, and that perspective can limit potential opportunities. Or an HR executive could be focused on employees only, and this can limit strategic potential.

Gathering data is valuable, but it's only as valuable as the context needed to make the best use of the data.

This is where the "human perspective" is so crucial for creating the future of work—if decisions are based solely on data and not with human context, we are missing the opportunity to make massive change through business.

In the ideate phase, the team at NextMapping™ includes insights and pattern interpretations with input from behavioral scientists and CIOs. Our team then interprets all of the data from a long list of possible perspectives.

A partial list of the perspectives we use to evaluate data includes:

» Customer perspective

» Employee perspective

» Leadership perspective

» Brand perspective

» Competitor perspective

» Environmental perspective

» Diversity perspective

» Generational perspective and more

We present our "holistic panoramic view" of the data, and we re-introduce leaders and teams to the organization through an updated, outside, and extensive multiple-perspectives lens.

In the ideate phase, the value is in the outside multiple perspectives of data and of an external consultancy to interpret and bring a new view of the company through outside eyes.

Once the data has been contextualized through the ideate phase, the next stage is "model."

Model – Now that the organization and the leaders have data and updated context of the organization through the discover and ideate stages, leaders and teams are able to have a next-level and expanded understanding of the organizational opportunities.

In this phase, we identify the "why" change needs to happen, the consequences of not making required changes, and a look at the research that affects the future potential of changes.

We identify current and future objectives, scope, players, and work areas including, "who does what" and why.

We conduct extensive research into the trends affecting the client, and we look at overall trends, including industry-specific trends. Building from both emerging and future trends supported by research data we integrate the data. From the previous steps of discover and ideate, now we "model" how the organization can think about actions and goals toward creating the future of the workplace.

We collaborate with research institutes and university research to find the most current information on emerging trends. In the model phase, we present the research in an infographic format to provide a visual reference point for where the research is pointing.

After the research phase, communicated via infographic, into emerging and future trends, we move on in the NextMapping™ process toward the "iterate" phase:

Iterate – Equipped with a researched contextual framework for the future of work for your organization, the next phase is interaction with the information that has been gathered and presented.

Through online polling, live polling, interviews, and one-on-one conversations held remotely and in person, we invite interaction with the data to add buy-in from leaders and teams and higher-level context as it applies to the organization on a cultural basis.

We ask, "What does all of this data mean to you in your job and for the company overall?"

We compile the responses and create a "story" of the organization of past, present, and future. We present that story as part of the map that is created.

Through feedback and multiple interpretations of the data, we now have a thorough "future view" of the organization that is 360 degrees.

Map – This is where our team at NextMapping™ distills all of the data gathered and what it ultimately means for the future of your organization, your leaders, your teams, and your clients. We convert the facts into a process map.

We connect the dots of all the research and data we gathered, clearly mapping out a number of strategic options for leaders and teams to take action on to create a future of work vision for your business and culture.

The map is a one-page visual "roadmap" that gives a clear outline of past successes, current successes, and future opportunities to leverage success. We add the contextualized data that has been assimilated and provide you with very clear options to be integrated into your strategic plans and goals.

The map can contain strategic areas identified, such as new technology, updated HR processes or solutions, innovation opportunities, and more.

The map is a one-page project plan that serves as both a guideline as well as a reference tool for every person within the organization. One of the biggest challenges in leading transformation is having everyone on the same page, driving in the same direction.

Having a visual roadmap provides ongoing confirmation of direction and a project management tool toward creating sustained success of the business.

The last phase of the NextMapping™ process is the "integrate" phase.

Integrate – We have created your future of work "NextMap," and now it's time to implement. The information and context are only as valuable as the ability to get everyone within the organization aligned and willing to implement the plans.

In the integrate phase, we outline the actionable steps toward creating the vision of the future within your organization. The map can be implemented by your leaders and teams as a project, or we partner with the organization to ensure project management and outside perspective on the entire process. When we help work through the map, we challenge each action/step (what/why? who/why? where/why? when/why? how/why?)

At this stage, we conduct an updated strategy session to line up the data NextMapping™ has gathered and strategize with leaders and teams using the NextMapping™ road map to complete the project plan, including priorities, timelines, actions, milestones, and goals.

We help you conduct an "all-hands" meeting that is both in person and virtual (for remote workers) and present the overall inspired vision for the future, roadmap in various formats, such as posters for in office, screen savers for all computers, laminated posters for desks, and on the wall and within the intranet or shared platforms used in the company.

The integrate phase includes one-on-one meetings with identified influencers, or "change leaders," to ensure connection and inspiration for their part of the plan. Included in the integration phase are videos created by the executive to speak to each part of the road-mapped plan to show both endorsement, buy-in, and support for the "future of work" plan.

From there we equip the leaders with a comprehensive "coach plan" to be used in conjunction with the communicated NextMapping™ plan. Leaders are encouraged to conduct weekly or bi-weekly one-on-ones with their team members to support, guide, and provide resources to assist teams in implementing the plan.

The coach plan includes:

» The change cycle to guide team members through change leadership—to be used as a self-assessment tool as to being "change ready" and toward being a "change leader."

» The transformational future-of-work mindset model, which is used as an accountability tool for ensuring the focus is on learning and sharing with teams and identifying when stuck in personal level or blame level.

» Access to our current online programs as learning and resources.

» The creation of real-time performance evaluation and process for this will be determined as a custom solution based on results of overall discovery, ideate, and model parts of the NextMapping™ process.

» Strategies on how to motivate, inspire, and engage employees in ongoing change and focus on future of work.

» Measurement guidelines to measure success in implementation of updated NextMapping™ plan.

» Reports back to leaders/organization on success of coaching and team success—measurements are based on real data, such as sales increase and customer retention as well as anecdotal and cultural shifts noted during the implementation phase.

During the integrate phase we develop/install new methods where we look at eliminating duplications, eliminate unnecessary work, combine steps, rearrange steps, and add new steps where needed.

To conclude and bring the entire NextMapping™ process full circle, we conduct end-of-project surveys to provide measurement on "then and now" and to identify key success factors and areas of continued opportunity.

Your company may already be doing parts of the NextMapping™ process, and you could be on the leading edge of change for your industry. Or perhaps your company is mid-way through an entire transformation process.

Here is a future-of-work checklist to see where you and your company are in creating the future of work:

- » Your company has a strategic plan that includes a specific focus on innovation and transformation of business for the next few years.

- » Your leaders are completely aligned with making all the changes needed in order to stay on the leading edge of success for the business.

- » Your teams are inspired, engaged, and are willingly implementing changes needed to drive transformation of the business.

- » Your culture is one of change leadership and innovation—everyone takes full responsibility for his or her success and for contributing to the company's success.

- » Your executives "walk the talk" in regard to innovating, encouraging innovation, and rewarding innovation.

- » Your culture rewards and recognizes entrepreneurial approaches to challenges and opportunities.

- » Your company has a well-laid-out plan related to succession, talent development, talent recruitment, and retention.

- » Your company has remote workers and a remote worker policy and provides flexible work options for workers.

- » Your company hires outsourced freelancers, contract workers, and other experts to work on projects.

» Your leaders are actively communicating, inspiring, and engaging all teams in the progress of change and updating on all information pertinent to transformation of the business.

» Your culture supports all workers in providing learning, mentoring, and coaching for success.

» Your culture has eliminated siloes through collaborative technologies and simplified processes that allow cross-functional information sharing, project input, and innovation opportunities.

» Your company has identified technology tools needed and has invested in them or will be investing in the near future.

» Your company is a shared leadership culture and "people first" in that the focus is on making people happy, including clients and employees

» Your leaders have the most up-to-date and relevant leadership skills that enable him or her to lead teams with inspiration, innovation, and collaboration.

If there is any one single item on the checklist that needs attention, you have an opportunity to lead the change toward transforming your job, your team, and ultimately your company.

The future we create is a very human future—as mentioned at the beginning and throughout this book, the future we create must be about people first and technology as the enabler to creating outstanding solutions for the betterment of people.

Back to the future day of work that we opened with in Chapter One:

You wake up the next day and your implanted biochip (an upgrade from the smart mirror in your bathroom) has already emitted the signal to your smart kitchen, where your latte is being made, your breakfast is being made, and your news of the day and update on global events is being recited to you while you eat.

Your smart wear (technology-enabled clothing) is synced with your implanted biochip and tells you daily how much you weigh, your nutritional update, and what and how much you need to eat for you to maintain optimal health.

You beam into the holoconference you signed up for to listen to the robot and human panel on industry updates. You continue viewing and listening to the conference while getting into your autonomous car that takes you on your way to your supersonic flight that takes you four hours to get anywhere in the world. In this scenario, you go from Vancouver to Shanghai, where you meet with partners about a possible merger, and you fly back the next day and it's as if you have never been gone from your home time zone. Your implanted chip helps regulate time zones so that you have zero jet lag and are able to function at full capacity no matter where you travel.

All of this work-related activity happens over a two-day period, and you are free to enjoy leisure time for the remaining five days of the week. In your leisure time, you are able to play games with your family, both in person and holographical, so no matter where in the world your family is spread out you can connect regularly.

In addition, the health and well-being of humans will be at its best in that the implanted microchip lets you know when it's time to talk to a support person or therapist and keeps you on track with your customized food and exercise program.

Relationships will be improved due to enhanced abilities to share feelings, communicate, and understand human development. Family time will be the measure of success in the future.

Workplaces will be a place of purpose, a place where everyone's unique skills are valued and integrated for the benefit of creating new technologies that transform the world and tackle problems such as poverty, lack of access to resources in third world countries, education availability for everyone on the planet, and more.

A VERY HUMAN FUTURE:

A <u>Korn Ferry</u> report says that there is a strong case based on research that the future of work is going to involve and very much include humans. Evidence suggests that humans will be indispensable and integral to creating an abundant future.

It's human talent, not technology or anything else, that is key to innovation and increasing growth. The World Economic Forum founder, Klaus Schwab, says that we are not in a race between humans and machines, rather that we are entering a future where humans will realize their FULL potential.

Experts state that humans will become only more valuable as technological innovation increases. It will be humans who will contextualize data, inspire others, and drive success.

Humans will delegate to technology to do the jobs that we find hard, and humans will do the jobs that humans are designed to do.

https://nextmapping.com/nextmapping-infographics-download/

AFTERWORD

JOIN THE NEXTMAPPING™ MOVEMENT – SHARE THE FUTURE YOU ARE CREATING

We invite you to join the NextMapping™ movement—we want you to share the future you are creating, either as an individual, with your team, as a leader, or as an organization.

Before any person can impact the future, he or she must be willing to be a change leader toward creating a new and better future. Before an organization can create greater impact for the future, there must be a culture of change leadership.

A change leader is someone focused on building on current success and creating a new and abundant future for self and others.

All leaders must have a vision for the future and the ability to communicate it in a way that creates buy-in and a desire for teams to follow.

Keep in mind that leaders do not create the future by themselves—it's a team effort, and it's a collaboration. If we go by the premise that in the future everyone will need to have leadership ability, then that means the future will have most of us in line with an agreed-upon vision for the future.

Let's join together to share innovative ideas, collaborative ideas, and case studies of inspirational people just like you changing the future of work!

Join me on <u>LinkedIn,</u> and I invite you to join our NextMapping™ group, where we share research, updates from people just like you, focused on creating the future, and more.

Join us also on Twitter at <u>@cherylcran</u> and <u>@nextmapping</u> for all things future of work.

We are also on <u>Facebook</u>—we post articles, blogs, research, and more.

RESOURCES

http://www.nextmapping.com

https://business.linkedin.com/content/dam/me/learning/en-us/pdfs/
lil-guide-attract-retain-top-tech-talent.pdf

https://www.glassdoor.com/employers/blog/attract-top-talent/

https://theundercoverrecruiter.com/top-talent-using-ai/

https://futurism.com

https://singularityhub.com/#sm.00001xya620pucdv5ypkgyih16xj4

https://www.weforum.org

https://nextmapping.com/the-future-of-work-online-courses/

https://www.headspace.com

https://choosemuse.com/

https://twitter.com/MuseumofRobots

https://www.trendhunter.com

https://changes-of-tomorrow.hyperisland.com

https://www.witi.com/articles/1436/Three-Trends-in-Human-
Behavior-Impacting-the-Future-of-Work/

https://www.pwc.com/gx/en/services/people-organisation/
publications/workforce-of-the-future.html

INDEX